Some of the wonders of Bordeaux

1 Les Halles de Bacalan and the Cité du Vin
(see page 109)

2 Château Lynch-Bages and the village of Bages
(see page 68)

3 The medieval centre of St-Emilion (see page 96)

4 Arcachon Bay and the Dune du Pilat
(see page 111)

5 The legendary D2, the Route des Châteaux
(see page 103)

6 Pessac-Léognan, the Garden of Bordeaux
(see page 88)

7 Entre-Deux-Mers – medieval towns and ancient monuments
(see page 100)

8 The sweet wine estates of Sauternes (see page 98)

All prices are correct at time of going to
press, but are subject to change.

Published 2024 by Académie du Vin Library Ltd
academieduvinlibrary.com
Founders: Steven Spurrier and Simon McMurtrie

Publisher: Hermione Ireland
Series editor: Adam Lechmere
Editor: Jon Richards
Copy editor: Katie Dicker
Design: Dan Prescott, Imago Create
Maps supplied by Cosmographics
Index: Marie Lorimer
Proofreader: Jenny Sykes
ISBN: 978-1-917084-51-2
Printed and bound in the EU
© 2024 Académie du Vin Library Ltd

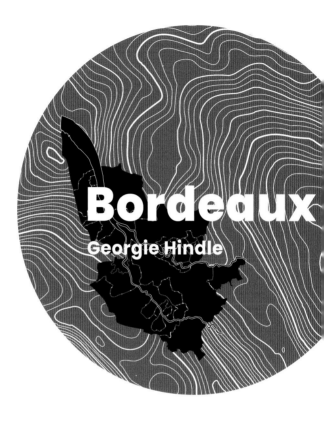

Bordeaux

Georgie Hindle

THE SMART TRAVELLER'S
WINE GUIDE

Contents

see page 28   see page 45

see page 87   see page 146

The fine neo-gothic towers of Château de Pressac,
St-Emilion Grand Cru Classé

Château Margaux

Foreword

The name Bordeaux is so evocative, its wines so renowned, you might think you know it already. For many, mention of Bordeaux conjures a picture of the grand châteaux of the Left Bank, with their legendary names – Lafite, Mouton, Margaux, Latour. That image might extend to the enchanting village of St-Emilion and its remarkable estates, among them Angelus, Cheval Blanc, Pavie and Ausone.

Bordeaux is one of the world's largest wine regions – over 9,000 châteaux and 100,000 hectares of vineyard – and home to some of the world's finest wines. From St-Estèphe to Sauternes, Pomerol to Pessac-Léognan, this diverse area is full of charming places to visit. Pessac-Léognan, dating back to the 4th century and listed as a UNESCO World Heritage Site, is the oldest Bordeaux terroir; it's an appellation blessed by the gods for many reasons.

Did you know that some of the finest wines in the region – including the world-renowned Château Haut-Brion – are produced here? Both the red and the white wines of this appellation are exceptional, delighting connoisseurs with their balance and freshness.

This part of Bordeaux is an oasis of green, rolling vineyard hills and woods with delightful shaded clearings. These breathtaking landscapes invite you, the visitor, to wander and savour an unforgettable experience.

All of Bordeaux welcomes visitors, but in Pessac-Léognan we like to think our welcome is warmer than most. We love to host visitors at our estates (where most of us live with our families). This lovely corner of Bordeaux is both diverse and unique. It embodies Bordeaux elegance – as we say, 'Pessac-Léognan, l'Esprit Bordeaux'.

This remarkable book is the beginning of your journey of discovery – not just of our appellation, but of the whole of Bordeaux.

Bon voyage!

Séverine Bonnie
Pessac-Léognan
Séverine Bonnie is a member of the Bonnie family, owners of Château Malartic-Lagravière since 1997

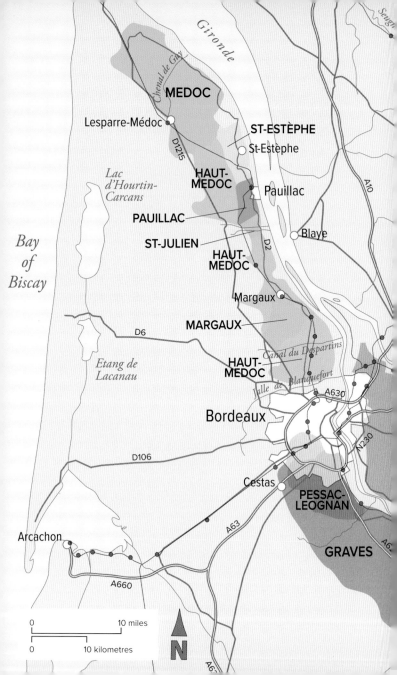

Gironde

MEDOC

Lesparre-Médoc

Chenal de Guy

D1215

Lac
d'Hourtin-
Carcans

ST-ESTÈPHE

St-Estèphe

HAUT-
MEDOC

Pauillac

PAUILLAC

Bay
of
Biscay

ST-JULIEN

Blaye

D2

HAUT-
MEDOC

Margaux

MARGAUX

D6

Etang de
Lacanau

Canal du Despartins

HAUT-
MEDOC

Jalle de Blanquefort

A630

Bordeaux

D106

N230

Cestas

PESSAC-
LEOGNAN

Arcachon

A63

GRAVES

A6

A660

Sevgn

A10

0   10 miles

0   10 kilometres

N

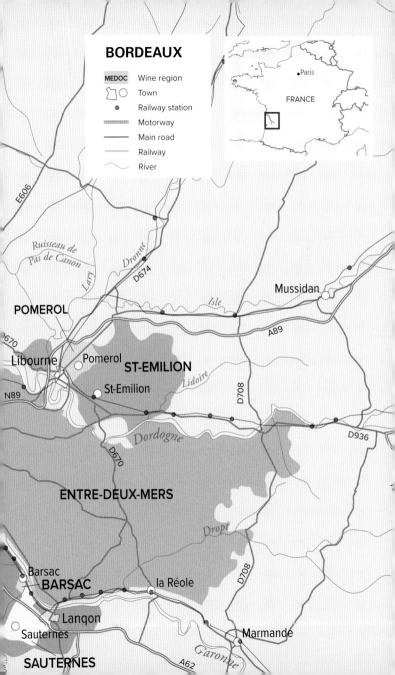

BORDEAUX

| MEDOC | Wine region |
| Town |
| Railway station |
| Motorway |
| Main road |
| Railway |
| River |

• Paris

FRANCE

E606

Ruisseau de Pas de Canon

Lary

Dronne

D674

Isle

Mussidan

POMEROL

A89

D670

Libourne

Pomerol

ST-EMILION

St-Emilion

Lidoire

D708

N89

Dordogne

D670

D936

ENTRE-DEUX-MERS

Dropt

D708

Barsac

BARSAC

la Réole

Lançon

Sauternes

Marmande

Garonne

A62

SAUTERNES

Introduction

Every wine region is unique, but Bordeaux has its own special place in the imagination. It's not the cradle of wine – many believe Georgia has that distinction – but it is the spiritual home of wine just as Hollywood is the home of film. This vast and infinitely varied corner of France epitomizes wine, even to those who have never pulled a cork.

From the humblest *petit château* on the fringes of St-Emilion to the magnificent estates of the Médoc, the word 'Bordeaux' on a wine label has a world of meaning – historical, cultural, social, gastronomic, scientific – to whoever happens to have picked up the bottle.

As Séverine Bonnie says in her foreword, so evocative is the name, so renowned are the wines, 'you might think you know Bordeaux already'. Often that knowledge is pure romance: Bordeaux means the fairytale turrets of Château Palmer, the glamour of Angelus or the unattainable perfection of a great vintage of Pétrus.

For many, no visit to Bordeaux would be complete without a selfie in front of the palladian splendour of Château Margaux (not for nothing is it called 'the Versailles of the Médoc'), and a genuflection at Haut-Brion. Others want to explore, to drive down tree-lined lanes in the Graves, or stay at a family-run winery in the Entre-Deux-Mers. Or you might prefer to spend your time in the bars and cafés of Bordeaux city itself, with the odd day trip to Pessac or St-Emilion.

We've tried to cater for every type of visitor to Bordeaux, whether you're a connoisseur wanting the coolest place with the best wine list, or just wine-curious.

Here you'll find Michelin-starred restaurants and brilliant wine bars, dozens of châteaux to visit, to stay in or to dine in, wine shops, wine routes and much more.

This is a book for anyone who wants not just to *visit* but to know and love the greatest wine region on Earth.

History

Bordeaux's Roman wines

The long and illustrious history of winemaking and viticulture in Bordeaux dates back thousands of years. The region first attracted settlers as early as the Bronze Age, around the 4th or 3rd centuries BCE. In the 1st century CE the Romans conquered Gaul; Bordeaux has been a flourishing town and port, particularly important to Spain and Britain, since then.

St-Emilion

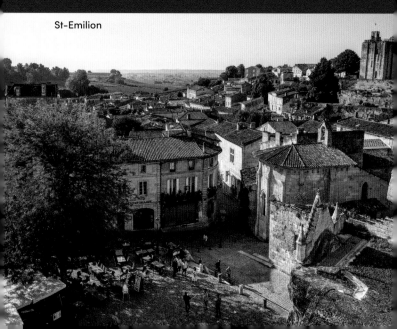

An ancient Celtic tribe known as the Bituriges Vivisci, which dwelt in the Bordeaux region in the 1st century CE, is part of the origin story of winemaking in Bordeaux. Archaeological evidence suggests that vines were cultivated along the banks of the Garonne River and its tributaries at around the same time. The Romans laid the foundations of Bordeaux's modern-day wine industry, bringing significant advancements in winemaking, and introducing new grape varieties, vineyard management techniques and practices.

The first written mention of wine is in the 4th century: the poet Ausonius, a native of Aquitaine, spoke of his homeland as a 'country for Bacchus, its river(s) and its great men'. In poems and letters he talks of his vines and of the Médoc, and his love of Pauillac. St-Emilion's renowned Château Ausone is said to be named after him.

Other documents and historical finds date vineyard cultivation to Roman times; grape-picking knives have been unearthed in Libourne, grape seeds have been found in ancient subsoils and fermentation bowls found buried in country villas.

The Middle Ages and English influence

During the Middle Ages, Bordeaux established itself as one of the pre-eminent wine-producing regions of Europe. Monastic orders in the region played a crucial role in preserving and expanding viticulture in Bordeaux; monasteries in St-Emilion and Sainte-Croix-du-Mont were important centres of vine cultivation and winemaking. In 1152, the marriage of the powerful Eleanor of Aquitaine to Henry Plantagenet (later Henry II of England) brought Aquitaine – an area stretching 3,000km from the foothills of the Massif Central in the north to the Pyrenees and the Spanish border in the south – under English control. This great region was renowned for its fertile lands, rich resources and strategic importance. Henry and his heirs sought to extract the maximum benefits from their new territory, including its fine vineyards – this was a time when the British were among the most enthusiastic consumers of wine in Europe. In order to guarantee Bordeaux's allegiance to the English crown, merchants were sweetened with tax breaks and trading rights, like the 'Bordeaux privilege', which forbade the shipping of any wine apart from Bordeaux before the feast of St Martin on November 11th. The royal court in London enthusiastically embraced Bordeaux, further boosting the region's reputation. Aquitaine became known as 'the wine cellar of England'.

This lucrative monopoly lasted some 300 years, a period of prosperity that was to end with the Battle of Castillon in 1453, during the final stages of the Hundred Years' War. The battle saw the victory of French forces and the consolidation of French sovereignty over Gascony and Bordeaux. Britain retained Calais but its influence in the rest of continental France was at an end.

After the English left, trade opened up. The Dutch in particular were interested in turning the region's white wines into eau-de-vie or brandy, which could survive long voyages to the tropics, where Dutch trading posts were established in the 16th and 17th centuries. Exports of wine and brandy boomed during these years with the majority of exported goods finding homes in the northern countries and American colonies.

Bordeaux harbour in the 18th century
by Claude-Joseph Vernet

In the 16th century the Dutch began to settle in Bordeaux, ushering in a 300-year period of influence known as the 'Dutch Golden Age'. Their engineers, experts in reclaiming land from the sea, drained vast areas of the marshy Médoc and made the region suitable for viticulture. They revealed the rocky, mineral-rich, gravel soils, similar to the Graves, where the most expensive wines of the day were grown. Winemakers quickly realized these well-draining soils were perfect for Cabernet Sauvignon. This was the basis for the fine wines that would go on to consolidate Bordeaux's reputation throughout the world.

The Dutch also developed efficient shipping routes, storage facilities and distribution networks, further aiding the international trade of Bordeaux wines.

British merchants set up in Bordeaux

After some years of trade disputes between England and France, by the end of the 1700s trade had been re-established, helped on the one hand by the bourgeoisie, many of whom were members of Bordeaux's parliament, affluent burghers with the means to plant and maintain vineyards. On the other hand, trade was boosted by a landowning aristocracy in England attracted by a lucrative market in Bordeaux.

All that remained was a merchant class who could facilitate the purchasing, storage and exportation of the 'New French Claret'. This was a style of wine that was becoming more and more popular, particularly when it came from the Médoc, where estates had seen changes in winemaking techniques and vineyard management practices. Vine training and pruning had evolved to optimize grape quality and yield. Oak barrels were installed for fermentation and ageing to improve structure, complexity and longevity; more attention was paid to the blends, resulting in wines with depth and distinctive regional character. Foreign merchants – notably German and British – arrived and set up in premises in the Chartrons suburb of Bordeaux, facing the Garonne River. Nathaniel Johnston (1734) of Château Ducru-Beaucaillou, and Schröder and Schÿler (1739) were two such *négoces*. The Irish arrived at the same time, waves of Catholics escaping Protestant persecution. Many joined the wine trade – the roll call of great Bordeaux estates is peppered with Irish names: Phélan Ségur, Boyd-Cantenac, Léoville Barton, Langoa Barton, Kirwan, Lynch-Bages, Pontac-Lynch, Lynch-Moussas, Dillon and Clarke.

The négociant system

In Bordeaux's complex way of doing business, négociants are the link between wine producers and consumers. They're basically distributors, and they've been around forever. During the Middle Ages their role was to act as intermediaries, purchasing wines from multiple châteaux, blending them as needed and distributing them to their network of domestic and international clients and buyers (to give an idea of how old the négociant system is, Louis IX tried to license them in 1243). Sourcing wine from several estates spread financial risk, reducing exposure to fluctuations in supply and demand. Négociants at the time also played a crucial role in maintaining quality standards. They became adept at blending wines with specific characteristics and flavour profiles.

By the 18th century, a centralized marketplace for wine transactions and negotiations was created: La Place de Bordeaux. The *Place* has never been a physical location; it is a virtual marketplace where producers (châteaux) can offer their wines for sale, and merchants (négociants) can purchase them, before offering them to wine merchants around the world. The *Place* today consists of some 300 négociants selling wine to merchants in around 170 countries. Some – Joanne, CVBG, Duclos, Grands Chais de France, Castel, Baron Philippe de Rothschild – are huge, multinational operations, dealing not just with Bordeaux wine but with fine wine from many different countries, such as Chile, Australia, the US, Italy and South Africa. Being listed on the *Place* is seen by many as a badge of honour.

To make things more complicated, another level of intermediary evolved: *courtiers*, or wine brokers. These slightly shadowy figures worked with châteaux and négociants, covering miles on horseback, getting to know producers and their vineyards, as well as tasting and assessing the wines. They are still a valuable link between château and négociant.

Phylloxera

While vineyard practices were improving in the 1800s, vine pests and diseases hampered activity, and led to one of the most devastating periods in the history of viticulture.

Phylloxera is an insect that feeds on the roots of grapevines. Thought to have been transported to Europe in the 1850s on imported American vine cuttings, it disrupts the flow of water and nutrients to the vine causing stunted growth, leaf discolouration and eventually, death. Native American vines had developed resistance to phylloxera through mutation; European vines had no defence.

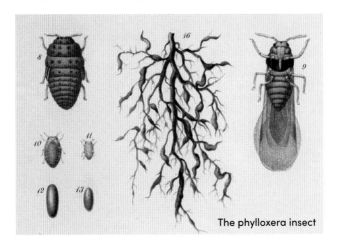

The phylloxera insect

Phylloxera cannot survive in sandy soils so Bordeaux's high-density vineyards on sandy and gravelly soils were mostly spared. Limestone and deep clay soils provided ideal conditions for phylloxera to spread quickly. By the middle of the 1870s, over 40% of French vineyards had been devastated. It was a catastrophe.

Many ultimately futile remedies – chemical treatments, soil fumigation and even flooding – were tried. All were unsuccessful until a Missouri entomologist put forward the idea of grafting European grapevine cuttings onto phylloxera-resistant American rootstocks. It was deeply divisive for obvious reasons: surely a Bordeaux Cabernet Sauvignon growing from an American-rooted vine would taste different? But it was found to work, and although it took two decades, by the beginning of the 20th century the vineyards had recovered.

By the early 1900s, a system of geographical indications and quality control was established by French law. The AOC (*Appellation d'Origine Contrôlée*) system was intended to regulate and protect the production of wine in specific regions. It was established in Bordeaux in 1936.

It defines the boundaries in which certain wines can be made, as well as the regulation of viticultural practices and winemaking techniques tailored to the specific characteristics of the terroir and grape varieties grown in that area.

The post–World War I slump

In the first decades of the 20th century the devastation of war, economic instability and changing consumer preferences led to a significant slump in Bordeaux's wine industry.

While wine remained the preserve of the wealthier classes, Bordeaux still suffered from the loss of export markets, Prohibition in the US, and a general movement away from traditional, high-priced Bordeaux wines towards lighter, more approachable and affordable styles.

Château Léoville Barton

The period of expansion and high production experienced prior to World War I, driven by increased demand and favourable market conditions, led to a surplus of wine in Bordeaux's cellars with merchants struggling to sell excess inventory in a shrinking market. Quality suffered, given the lack of labour and reduced investment, further undermining Bordeaux's reputation. Looking at the manicured lawns and graceful weeping willows of Château Lafite, say, it's hard to imagine how different Bordeaux was in the 1950s. When the late Anthony Barton (he died in 2022) moved to St-Julien from Ireland in 1951 to work with his uncle Ronald at the family properties Léoville Barton and Langoa Barton, he endured leaking roofs and hopeless plumbing; the business was running at a loss and one more poor harvest would force them to sell, Ronald Barton said. Today, the Bartons are among the most celebrated of the Médoc châteaux.

As the 1950s wore on, as in much of Europe, Bordeaux's wine industry was faced with rebuilding and modernizing with efforts made to rehabilitate vineyards, replant vines, restore winemaking facilities and capitalize on advances in technology and viticultural practices.

A more globalized marketplace embraced new distribution channels and Bordeaux benefited from an expansion in export markets; North American sales helped offset declining interest in Europe. Bordeaux already had a rich history in America. Thomas Jefferson, founding father and third President, was a Francophile and a powerful advocate for Bordeaux, a passion he'd nurtured since his years as American ambassador in Paris. He travelled several times to Bordeaux and bought a good deal of wine to be shipped home. Indeed, he may well have been the first great wine bore. 'There was, as usual, a dissertation upon wines. Not very edifying,' John Quincy Adams wrote in his diary after dining with Jefferson in 1807.

Bordeaux became increasingly popular in the latter half of the 20th century, but it was the 1982 vintage and the effusive style of a home-produced newsletter (it was little more than a fanzine at first) called Wine Advocate, the brainchild of American lawyer-turned-critic Robert Parker, that ushered in the new era. It might almost be called the Age of Parker.

Robert Parker 'could make or break a reputation'

1982 and the rise of Robert Parker

Considered one of Bordeaux's greatest-ever vintages, 1982 produced a plentiful crop of ripe, generous and rich wines that ushered in a new style of opulent Bordeaux but it also propelled Parker onto the international stage.

Parker had released the first issue of the (then free) bi-monthly in 1978 so he had a solid following. By enthusiastically endorsing 1982, when august critics in America and Europe were saying it was too ripe and wouldn't stay the course, he gained a much wider audience. Over the years, the 82 has gone on to become one of the most famous Bordeaux vintages. Parker called it right.

Part of his appeal was his new scoring system. While the *Wine Advocate* wasn't the first consumer-facing wine publication, Parker was the first to use the 100-point wine rating scale, which became widely adopted in the US and throughout the wine industry.

Parker's reviews and ratings placed a strong emphasis on the quality of Bordeaux wines and those who received favourable scores were rewarded with increased recognition and sales, encouraging a focus on quality and consistency in winemaking practices. During the 2000s, Parker could wreck or make a reputation. Analysis of his scores on the 2005 vintage showed that for a St-Emilion Grand Cru, each additional point above 90 was worth an extra £201 per case.

Not only did Parker champion smaller estates, he disrupted the given hierarchy of Bordeaux properties, particularly away from the Médoc, with a strong focus on St-Emilion and Pomerol. While Parker's ratings brought attention and acclaim to many Bordeaux estates, they also sparked criticism and controversy within the industry after it became clear he favoured a particular style of wine: ripe, fruit-forward, richly concentrated, high-alcohol with pronounced oak flavours.

The need to win 'Parker points' and the subsequent jump in sales spawned widespread production of this style of wine. It also prepared the ground for the 'garagiste' movement, which had its epicentre in St-Emilion. 'Garagiste' was coined by French wine critic Michel Bettane, who sniffed at innovative producers adopting non-traditional methods to produce small-scale batches of wines. The wines – the 1991 vintage of Valandraud is considered the first – were critically, even cultishly, acclaimed at the time. The hype they experienced in the early 1990s and 2000s has passed. Famous examples include Château Valandraud (by early pioneer Jean-Luc Thunevin), Le Dôme (Jonathan Maltus) and La Mondotte of Château Canon La Gaffelière (Stephan von Neipperg). Pomerol's two-hectare Le Pin, one of the world's most expensive wines, was actually made in a garage and is often also considered the inspiration for the movement, though owner Jacques Thienpont has little patience with such theories.

Methods to reduce yields and increase ripeness were introduced as well as using new oak for both extended maceration, fermentation and ageing to bolster the distinctive character and bold flavours of the resulting wines. Wine consultant Michel Rolland, who consulted for several of the movement's key producers, is closely associated with the garagiste movement (indeed, he's often mentioned in the same breath as Parker). The wine world has moved on: the term 'garagiste' is old-hat, and 'Parkerization', once ubiquitous, is seldom heard nowadays. Still, the movement was influential in that it challenged the dominance of Bordeaux's established châteaux, and contributed to a diversification of wine styles.

While Parker's influence on Bordeaux wines was profound, his impact has diminished in recent years with the rise of other critics and changing consumer preferences for less ripe, more elegant and fresh wines.

The boom years

Fuelled by increased international demand, rising prices and investments in vineyards and wineries, the 1990s into the 2000s marked a period of significant growth and expansion for Bordeaux. A wave of wealthy individuals, corporations and international investors arrived, chequebooks in hand, looking to buy up existing estates or create entirely new vineyard properties. The obvious focus was on prestigious appellations within the Médoc as well as St-Emilion and Pomerol on the Right Bank.

The Far East also came into play. The Japanese developed a strong appreciation for the wines as symbols of prestige and luxury. China also emerged as a major player, and, as its economy boomed and middle classes expanded, demand for luxury goods including wine soared. Owning, serving and gifting Bordeaux wines became synonymous with wealth and sophistication.

China emerged as a major player

Cité du Vin, Bordeaux

Château Lafite had been selling in China since 1992, and lost no time in capitalizing on the boom. Its Chinese name, which is considered easier to pronounce for the Chinese than the other First Growths, is a contributing factor to its success as well as its canny attention to the market. Prices of the second wine, Carruades de Lafite, can often command more than Second Growths and the entry-level Légende range also sells for extraordinary prices. In a bold move, Lafite also famously etched the Chinese symbol for the figure eight (the luckiest number in Chinese culture) on the 2008 bottles. Mouton also played up to the Chinese market by using famous artist Xu Lei to illustrate its 2008 label. Both wines initially soared in price.

2008 became a watershed year for the growth of the fine wine market in China. Taxes on wines imported to Hong Kong were reduced from 40% to zero, powering the Bordeaux boom. The Chinese appetite for Bordeaux wines, particularly after the 2008 financial crisis when the UK and US were struggling, saved Bordeaux; today, around 150 estates are Chinese owned.

The combination of growing international demand and limited supply drove up prices of Bordeaux during this period. Speculation in wines became increasingly common with buyers and collectors buying solely for investment.

En primeur also contributed to price increases, particularly with estates keen to capitalize on the Chinese willing to pay a premium for 'unfinished' wines. By early 2010, Hong Kong and Macau were the world's largest purchasers of Bordeaux.

However, the exceptional 2009 and 2010 vintages left a sour taste in the Far East thanks to a combination of record prices, and releases in tranches (where estates offer portions of their production for sale with incremental price increases – the first being the cheapest and most coveted but also the smallest). 'Bundling' wines was rife, with buyers required to buy cheaper wines in order to secure the top names. With speculative sales, those who bought in 2009 without profit questioned further purchases. The lure of buying the world's best wines and turning a quick and easy profit lost its lustre.

By 2012, Chinese buyers had turned their attention to Burgundy, attracted by greater trading rewards. In 2013, the Chinese government also cracked down on lavish gifting and entertainment as part of business negotiations. Outside of the Chinese market, good to average vintages followed for the next four years until the well-regarded 2015 *en primeur* campaign when only producers who lowered prices were rewarded. The 2019 vintage campaign was viewed as semi-prosperous but when looking at the 2017–2021 vintages, only a few wines show average positive returns since release.

Today the landscape is tough with Bordeaux battling the effects of the closure of the Chinese market to Western countries. Economic slowdowns, market saturation, reducing consumer purchasing power, trade disputes and diplomatic conflicts have all led to disruption in trade and commerce impacting Bordeaux wine exports to China.

Further afield, the precarious global economic situation, general political instability, the COVID-19 pandemic, climate change, Brexit, American trade tariffs, increased cost of living, changing consumer trends and drinking habits are all threatening Bordeaux. But the world's greatest wine region has survived far worse; it remains resilient, with wineries adapting to changing conditions and merchants seizing opportunities for export growth in new markets.

Bordeaux's classification systems

First Growths, 'Super Seconds', Thirds, Fourths and Fifths – what does it all mean, and why does it matter?

Château Latour's iconic tower

The 1855 classification

Arguably the best-known and most important wine classification in the world, the 1855 (as it's known) has stood the test of time.

The 1855 was initiated by Napoleon III to showcase the best wines of Bordeaux at the Exposition Universelle de Paris in 1855. It focused on the red wines from the Médoc, organising 61 estates into five tiers (known in French as Crus, or 'growths': the official ranking of Château Margaux is Premier Cru Classé en 1855, or First Growth Classified in 1855). The list was based on the prestige and market prices of the wines at the time; famously, Château Mouton Rothschild didn't make the cut, as the Rothschild family had only just bought it. Baron Philippe de Rothschild made it his life's work to get his property elevated, and finally succeeded in 1973.

The sweet wines of Sauternes were ranked by the same system but with only two tiers, and Château d'Yquem being given a special status of 'Premier Cru Supérieur'.

Although the 1855 is often criticized for being outdated (it's remained almost unchanged for 170 years), whenever some enterprising wine merchant crunches the numbers according to how well the wines perform in today's market, the result is a surprisingly similar list.

There are now five First Growths – the famous five are Château Lafite Rothschild, Mouton Rothschild (usually known simply as Lafite and Mouton), Latour, Margaux, and Haut-Brion (the only non-Médoc estate). There are 18 Second Growths, 14 Third Growths, 10 Fourth Growths and 18 Fifth Growths.

Although the 1855 is often criticized for being outdated (it's remained almost unchanged for 170 years), whenever some enterprising wine merchant crunches the numbers according to how well the wines perform in today's market, the result is a surprisingly similar list.

Accurate or outdated, the 1855 remains a hierarchy of excellence for Bordeaux lovers all over the world.

St-Emilion classification

It was another 100 years before St-Emilion was granted its own classification, in 1955. This differed in two major aspects from the 1855: ranking was decided on quality by a jury of wine professionals, and the list was to be updated every 10 years. The classification, the most recent being the seventh, in 2022, ranks châteaux into three categories: Premier Grand Cru Classé (A and B) and Grand Cru Classé. Currently it lists 85 properties, including 2 Premiers Grand Cru Classés A (Figeac and Pavie), 12 Premiers Grand Cru Classés and 71 Grand Cru Classés. The process relies heavily on the judgement of the individual members of the jury (they appraise terroir, vineyard management, winemaking techniques, the wine's reputation and its quality through a blind tasting of 10–15 vintages). It's been dogged by controversy since 2006, when a trio of châteaux protested their demotion. The entire listing was scrapped amid fierce debate, and not re-run until 2012. That, too, ended in tears, with a conviction and fine for one prominent owner. Before the 2022 classification, three out of the previous four top-ranked estates left the system altogether.

Château Malartic-Lagravière, Pessac-Léognan

The Graves classification

The Crus Classés de Graves classification was established in 1953, recognizing the top estates by the wines they make, either red, white or both; there's no hierarchy and no revision. The 16 estates which are considered to represent the pinnacle of Graves winemaking all belong to the small and friendly appellation Pessac-Léognan. The First Growth Château Haut-Brion is the only Bordeaux estate to be classified twice, appearing in both the Graves classification and the Grand Cru Classés of 1855. Other great properties include Château Smith Haut Lafitte, Domaine de Chevalier, Château Malartic-Lagravière, Château Pape Clément and Château La Mission Haut-Brion. These are world-renowned properties – many consider the white wines of Pessac-Léognan, blends of Sémillon and Sauvignon Blanc, to be the finest, and longest-lived, of their kind in the world. The prices they command bear this out.

The Cru Bourgeois classification

The Cru Bourgeois classification recognizes quality Médoc wines that were not included in the 1855 classification. Wines are evaluated by tastings and quality assurance and ranked either Cru Bourgeois, Cru Bourgeois Supérieur or Cru Bourgeois Exceptionnel.

First introduced in the 19th century, the Cru Bourgeois is updated every five years and (as is par for the course when it comes to Bordeaux rankings) it's not without controversy. For example, the Supérieur and Exceptionnel levels were dropped in 2007 after accusations of bias among the judges. They were reintroduced in 2020, but minus some names – châteaux including Poujeaux, Chasse Spleen, Sociando-Mallet, Potensac, Ormes de Pez, Phélan Ségur and Gloria – all internationally-renowned properties. Time will tell if the Cru Bourgeois is going to descend into acrimony à la St-Emilion, but for now it does provide a benchmark of quality for consumers.

What is a First Growth and a Super Second, and why it's useful to know

The great names of Bordeaux – Mouton Rothschild, Lafite, Margaux, Latour and Haut-Brion – have attained an almost mythical status over the centuries. There are few who would not recognize them as shorthand for luxury and vinous greatness. But how many know exactly what is meant by a First Growth – or, for that matter, a Super Second?

Lafite, with its 110 hectares of vineyard, is the largest of the five First Growths (see the 1855 classification page 29). It was established in the 13th century; Haut-Brion, dating back to Roman times, is the smallest at 53 hectares (three of which are white). Latour, founded in the 14th century, is the second largest with 92 hectares; Mouton, 15th century, has 83 hectares; Margaux, 16th century, has 82 hectares.

We list the vineyard hectarage because it gives a very good idea of the size of these operations. Only in Bordeaux could a 100-hectare estate produce wines of such stellar reputation. Consider France's other legendary wines: in Burgundy, for example, many estates are pocket-handkerchief in size. The greatest of them all, Domaine de la Romanée-Conti (DRC), owns around 31.5 hectares of

Château Ducru-Beaucaillou, St-Julien

vineyard, from which it makes 13 wines. DRC's smallest holding is half a hectare of Corton Clos du Roi Grand Cru. It makes Lafite look like a vast corporation.

While all five of the Bordeaux Firsts are family-owned, those families are wealthy and influential dynasties spanning generations, some with important businesses behind them. Lafite and Mouton are owned by two different branches of the Rothschild family; Latour by Artémis Domaines, owned by French billionaire François Pinault, head of luxury group Kering and worth some $40 billion; Haut-Brion is part of the Dillon empire, headed up by Prince Robert of Luxembourg; Margaux is owned by French-Greek businesswoman Corinne Mentzelopoulos, heiress to a shipping empire, and run by her children, third-generation Alexis and Alexandra.

'Only in Bordeaux could a 100-hectare estate produce wines of such stellar reputation'

Not all estates correlate to their Cru Classé designation; some rival or surpass their growth in terms of wine quality, market demand and prestige. This is unsurprising given that the 1855 rankings referred to the château itself rather than its vineyards. In the last 170 years, many properties have vastly expanded their vineyard holdings within the same appellation. Of the First Growths, only Haut-Brion and Margaux have the same vineyard holdings they had in 1855.

Super Second is an unofficial term which evolved in the late 20th century to describe a group of estates that consistently outperform their original 1855 classification. They often sell for more money than their counterparts, and are almost the same quality as the First Growths, but not as expensive. The list includes some existing Second Growths as well as a Third Growth (the consistently brilliant Château Palmer) and a Fifth Growth (Château Lynch-Bages). Other properties in the list include Cos d'Estournel, Léoville Las Cases, Léoville Barton and Pichon Comtesse.

The 18th-century Place de la Bourse, a symbol of Bordeaux's prosperity, now home to the Chamber of Commerce and the Musée National des Douanes

The *en primeur* system

En primeur is a system whereby wines are offered for sale while still in barrel: in short, the wines are sold as futures. They are tasted by (literally) thousands of the world's critics and merchants during two or three intense weeks in the spring (usually around Easter); the châteaux then decide how they are going to price the wines, and they release them to the négociants (see pages 18–19), who offer them to merchants, who then call – or WhatsApp – their clients.

En primeur is one of Bordeaux's busiest times – about 7,000 critics and merchants arrive for tastings, dinners and parties – and it's become increasingly controversial over the years. The idea is that it gives access to limited-production wines that are investment opportunities. Buyers speculate on the future value of the wines with the intention of reselling, particularly if critics like them or the vintage is a good one.

For the producers, the system provides an opportunity to gauge demand early in the production process, and allows them to secure cash flow before the wines are ready for release. It's a very neat way of keeping your books healthy.

Of course for merchants there are advantages to a system that gives early access to wines, but criticism is mounting: wine lovers and collectors especially make the point that there is little point in buying the wine now, when it will be the same price (or cheaper) a few years later.

Tasting very young wines isn't an exact science but the idea is that the consumer is getting a good deal – whether buying for cellaring and drinking, or for investment. But wine investment isn't as secure these days, fewer people have wine cellars and there are more interesting wines to try.

Château Latour famously removed itself from the *en primeur* system. But not everyone can afford to lose the opportunity to sell and secure cash at such an early stage. That said, only a small proportion of Bordeaux's total wine production is considered *en primeur*-worthy in terms of investment, with only 300 or so wines theoretically increasing in price by the time they're in bottle.

Love it or hate it, *en primeur* is an institution. There's too much money at stake for it to change (a big London merchant, in the heyday of Bordeaux, would sell £60 million of wine in the couple of months after prices are released). It's brilliant promotion for Bordeaux, it creates a sense of anticipation and drama, and for aspiring wine writers it's a crash course in how Bordeaux works. As one producer suggested, *en primeur* created the discipline of wine writing; that, and the fact that thousands of critics end up writing about hundreds of wines that aren't sold as futures (and that might not have got recognition), can only be a good thing.

Geography

Bordeaux, the capital of the Gironde *département*, sits in a low-lying basin where two rivers, the Dordogne and the Garonne, meet to form the great Gironde, which widens into a vast, cool estuary on its journey north to the Atlantic Ocean.

Le Pont de Pierre, Bordeaux

This great tidal body of water – the largest estuary in Europe and a natural harbour – is lined with majestic sights, including 10 lighthouses, the 17th-century Blaye citadel, troglodyte caves and more than 40 ports. It's also the only estuary in the world where European sturgeon travel to breed.

The influence of the Gironde estuary on the development of the vineyards of Bordeaux is crucial. The Gironde has for centuries served as a vital transport artery, allowing seagoing vessels – via the Garonne – to reach the port of Bordeaux; it is also part of the great Canal des Deux Mers, the east-to-west waterway that links the Mediterranean and the Atlantic. An essential hub for shipping and trade since ancient times, the Gironde has been crucial to the export of Bordeaux wines, contributing to the city's prosperity. This massive body of water, constantly moved by four daily tides, regulates the temperature in the vineyards, cooling the land in the summer and moderating the Bordeaux winter.

Atlantic climate

Every second, 18 bottles of wine with 'Bordeaux' on the label are sold around the world. This is one of the world's largest wine regions, representing 20% of all of France's vineyards. This vast area – stretching over 130km from north to south, with some 110,000 hectares under vine – produces around 650 million bottles a year. Languedoc-Roussillon to the south produces more wine from twice as much vineyard, but judged on the value of its wines, Bordeaux is the most significant fine-wine region on Earth.

Bordeaux, located on the 45th parallel, has a temperate climate, with warm summers and mild winters. This is the effect of the Gulf Stream, which contributes to moisture and humidity. However, when it comes to the vine, it's far more complicated than that.

Bordeaux scholar and wine expert Jane Anson notes in her seminal book *Inside Bordeaux* that the region has five 'temperature zones' that affect the ripening and quality of grapes. Put simply, the valleys of the Garonne, Dordogne and Gironde are warmer, and these are the regions – the Médoc, St-Emilion and Pomerol, Sauternes – that produce the very finest wines.

For the visitor, Bordeaux's (usually) reliably sunny summer climate is ideal. For the vigneron, as ever, it's more complicated. Winters can be harsh, with frosts descending as late as the spring, while ferocious summer hailstorms are not uncommon. Both can have devastating consequences: frost in 2017 and hail in 2018 wiped out hundreds of vineyards. Miserable weather throughout July and August made 2011 a famously difficult year. Also notorious was 2013, with a damp and depressing spring, heavy storms in June, a near-hurricane in July that uprooted trees in the Médoc, and hail in August.

This variable climate contributes to the enduring fascination with the wines of Bordeaux. No matter how sophisticated 21st-century winemaking might be (and the

The famous D2 winds through the vineyards of the Médoc

top châteaux use the most expensive technology in the world), every winemaker is at the mercy of the weather. That's why every Bordeaux vintage is different to the last.

Production – and overproduction

Variable vintage conditions have a considerable effect on how much wine Bordeaux produces. Talk to anyone in the Bordeaux wine business – from grower and winemaker, to négociant or wine merchant – and it won't be long before they mention the crisis afflicting the region. There are many reasons for this, but they can be boiled down to a recent run of 'good' vintages (favourable weather bringing bumper harvests and high quality) coupled with difficult market conditions (worldwide, people are drinking less red wine); as a result, there's too much wine to sell. This affects cheaper, entry-level Bordeaux much more than the top wines, whose market is pretty stable. The solution is to make less wine, and in 2023 some 9,500 hectares of vines were uprooted. While this doesn't affect the most prestigious vineyards, which comprise only 5% of Bordeaux's output, it means that increasingly large numbers of winemakers are facing financial difficulties. The most favoured areas produce some of the greatest wines in the world, and they command high prices; in less exalted areas, there are many wine growers without the necessary means, incentives or physical ability to produce commercially viable wines.

A region of blends

Most of us have a good idea of what a 'classic' Bordeaux should be: a complex, delicate, age-worthy wine with fine tannins and delicate, balanced fruit flavours – the very opposite of a big, bold Australian wine, for example, with its exuberant fruit and soft tannins. But that's only a fraction of the story. Bordeaux produces a huge range of styles, each with its own characteristics: elegant, structured reds; crisp,

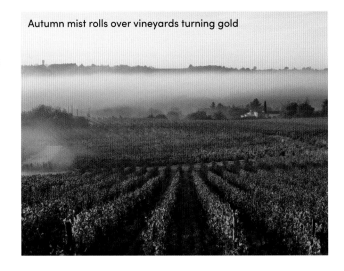

Autumn mist rolls over vineyards turning gold

aromatic whites; and rich, decadent dessert wines.

Unlike Burgundy, which produces single-varietal wines mainly from Pinot Noir or Chardonnay, Bordeaux is a multiple-variety region, and its winemakers are the world's master blenders. Bordeaux reds are typically made from a mix of Cabernet Sauvignon, Merlot, Cabernet Franc, Petit Verdot and Malbec, the proportions of which vary depending on where they are grown and who is making them. You might think Cabernet Sauvignon is the king of the region, but in fact almost three times as much Merlot is grown (70,000 hectares to Cabernet's 24,000).

White Bordeaux is typically made from a blend of Sauvignon Blanc and Sémillon, sometimes with smaller amounts of Muscadelle. These wines are known for their freshness, acidity and aromatic complexity, with flavours of citrus, stone fruit and herbal notes. They can range from crisp and light, to fuller-bodied with oak ageing, depending on the winemaking style.

Bordeaux also produces some of the world's most famous sweet wines. The great wines of Sauternes and

Barsac (with Château d'Yquem the most famous of all) are of legendary rarity and expense. They can be made only when the grapes are affected – in perfect conditions of humidity and heat – by noble rot, or *botrytis cinerea*, a fungus whose spores shrivel the grapes to a grey, mushy mess. They might be horrible to look at, but nobly rotted grapes retain thimblefuls of the most exquisitely sweet juice, resulting in wines capable of ageing hundreds of years, with luscious flavours of honey, apricot and marmalade, and tingling acidity.

Bordeaux's appellations

Bordeaux is divided into 65 *Appellations d'Origine Contrôlée* (AOCs), or protected designations of origin. This is a certification based on technique, expertize and the concept of terroir, which is fundamental to understanding wine and its connection to the land.

Famously untranslatable, terroir refers to the intricate interplay between natural and human influences on wine production. California winemaker Warren Winiarski describes it very simply as 'the three Gs: the Ground, the Grape and the Guy (or Gal)'. Environmental factors that affect the grapes (and the wines made from them)

Sémillon affected by noble rot, Sauternes

include soil type and composition, climate, topography (altitude, slope orientation and proximity to water) and the way the vine has adapted to specific conditions. Then there are the human factors: vineyard practices, farming methods and winemaking techniques.

Making a wine that expresses its terroir is the goal of any winemaker. 'I've tried, step by step, to make a link between the taste of the wine and the composition of the soil,' is how international consultant Stéphane Derenoncourt describes his life's work. Terroir-driven wines are supposed to give a sense of place: the gravelly soils of Pessac-Léognan, for example, should express themselves in a certain freshness, or leanness, in the wines; the heavier, clay-based soils of St-Emilion might produce wines that are soft and elegant.

Bordeaux vineyards are often defined as Left Bank and Right Bank, depending on whether they sit to the west or the east of the Gironde estuary and the two rivers that flow into it, the Garonne and the Dordogne. The Médoc and the Graves are Left Bank, while St-Emilion

and Pomerol are Right Bank. These distinctions represent different soils, different dominance of grape varieties and different winemaking styles.

The Médoc and the Graves, known for their gravelly soils, are primarily planted with the Cabernet Sauvignon, Merlot, Cabernet Franc, Petit Verdot and Malbec varieties. Left Bank wines are typically dominated by Cabernet Sauvignon, and they are known for their structure, depth and ageing potential. Some of the most prestigious vineyards are concentrated in the Médoc, particularly in the appellations of Pauillac, Margaux, St-Julien and St-Estèphe, the homes of such famed châteaux as Mouton Rothschild, Lafite Rothschild, Margaux, Palmer, Léoville Barton and many more.

The Right Bank includes the renowned subregions of St-Emilion and Pomerol, among others, known for their clay and limestone soils. This part of Bordeaux is primarily planted with Merlot, Cabernet Franc and smaller amounts of Cabernet Sauvignon and Malbec; the wines made here are known for their softness, elegance and approachability, often displaying ripe fruit flavours. Famous estates include Cheval Blanc, Pétrus, Ausone, Le Pin and Lafleur.

Selling Bordeaux

The best Bordeaux wines are highly commercialized, with great investment potential and a strong presence in international markets. They are often seen as a benchmark for quality, and their reputation has been bolstered by the attention of critics, collectors and enthusiasts worldwide.

To take just one example, in 2023 three cases of Château Lafite Rothschild 2000 (one of the most famous vintages of the last half-century) sold at auction for $34,000, a rise of 300% on what they were fetching in 2008.

However, there is plenty more wine to be enjoyed beyond the top estates and the most vaunted names. Certainly beyond the £30/$30 mark, Bordeaux offers the best value-to-ageability ratio of any wine in the world, with modestly priced bottles able to age more than 50 years.

Bordeaux has been adept at marketing its wines globally, with initiatives aimed at both connoisseurs and casual drinkers, but there is a sense today that Bordeaux isn't 'cool': the wines need to age 20 years before being approachable, and sommeliers would rather promote more diverse styles. Indeed, entry-level Bordeaux reds can seem light and meagre in comparison to the ripe and fuller-bodied versions from California, Australia and South Africa.

However, warmer weather, technical advances, investment and more environmentally conscious winemaking over the past decade mean that Bordeaux is producing the best wines in its history. A failure to sell all of its production is not down to quality alone; it is also due to competition in the form of 'value wines' from other regions and changing consumer habits.

Bordeaux remains one of the most dynamic wine regions in the world, with a vast majority of excellent, fresh and fruity wines that deserve their place on the table. Continuous evolution occurs in terms of precision viticulture, organic and biodynamic farming practices, mitigating climate change and the development of new markets. The region also hosts numerous wine events and festivals, and it is fast adapting to changing trends, technologies and consumer preferences. While Bordeaux embraces innovation, it also values heritage, and centuries-old histories and winemaking traditions passed down through generations continue to shape the region's identity and reputation.

Château Guiraud, Sauternes

The communes and their wines

There is really no such thing as a 'typical' Bordeaux. The differences between the terroirs of the appellations is so marked – the gravel of the Graves compared to the clay and limestone of St-Emilion, say – it's no wonder the wines are distinct in terms of style, taste and texture. Here we look at the character of the communes from north to south and east to west.

St-Emilion

Left Bank

St-Estèphe

St-Estèphe, in the far north of the Médoc, is known for powerful, tannic earthy reds with bold flavours of dark fruits and cedar. They're not as sweet and fruity as their more southerly counterparts and can be quite austere and tightly packed when young. This robust style comes from a mixture of soils including rocks, sand, clay, limestone and gravel; the soils contain more clay than in Pauillac, St-Julien or Margaux. Close to the Garonne, more hilly and undulating than the southern Médoc, it has a variety of microclimates. Many estates have incredible views of the vines sweeping down towards the estuary.

St-Estèphe is 60km from the city of Bordeaux, more than an hour's drive. It would have been a long day's journey by horse, and many think this remoteness from the centre of things contributed to the wines being judged unfairly at the 1855 classification. It's one of the largest of the Médoc communes but it has only five classified estates: two Second Growths, one Third, one Fourth and one Fifth Growth.

Amongst those five, there are exceptional estates with mighty reputations. The two Second Growths, Château Cos d'Estournel and Château Montrose, dominate although close behind is Château Calon Ségur, the most northerly of all classified estates and consistently among the best of the appellation. All three produce wines with huge ageing potential. Expect prices to reflect the quality, with top wines commanding significant sums.

There are also lots of excellent non-classified estates with some of the best Cru Bourgeois in Bordeaux. Top estates include Phélan Ségur (a Cru Bourgeois with a stellar reputation), de Pez, Les Ormes de Pez, Lilian Ladouys, de Côme and Haut-Marbuzet. The region's gravelly soils impart structure and depth to the wines, while the maritime influence moderates temperatures, contributing to the wine's elegance. The wines are known for their freshness, purity and tastes of graphite and wet-stone minerality.

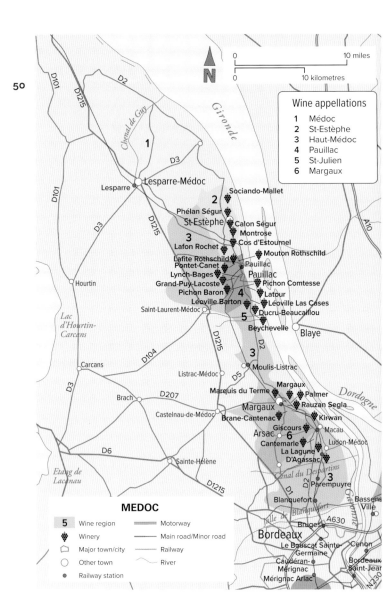

Some take years to open; the Cru Bourgeois wines are more approachable.

Pauillac

Pauillac, quintessential Cabernet country, its wines considered classic expressions of fine Bordeaux, has some of the most prestigious vineyards and sought-after wines in Bordeaux – and the world. Three out of the five First Growths – Lafite, Latour and Mouton – are in this appellation.

To the north of the appellation there are high elevations and deep gravels on top of sand, marl and limestone, to the south a greater concentration of larger, gravel rocks and stones with more clay in the subsoils. There are 18 Cru Classé estates that make up 84% of the appellation's production. This makes finding 'cheap' Pauillac somewhat difficult. It has three Firsts, two Seconds, one Fourth and 12 Fifth Growths – mainly located in the south of the appellation given the difference in soils to the north.

> ## 'Three out of the five First Growths – Lafite, Latour and Mouton – are in Pauillac'

Expect bold flavours of blackcurrant, cigar box and gravelly minerality, with firm tannins and a long, lingering finish. Outside of the top three, Second Growths Château Pichon Baron and Château Pichon Longueville Comtesse de Lalande (usually shortened to Pichon Comtesse) take the spotlight; Fifth Growths Lynch-Bages and Pontet-Canet can often command higher prices than their higher-classified neighbours. These two, alongside Lafite's sister winery Clerc Milon and Grand-Puy-Lacoste (GPL), which also produce excellent wines, would probably be upgraded were the classification to be redrawn.

St-Julien

Heading south, St-Julien is the smallest of the big four Médoc appellations, and has the highest concentration of family-owned estates. It has a terroir comprising gravel mounds and terraces over clay, sand and more rarely limestone with a microclimate influenced by the vineyards that have gentle slopes onto the Gironde estuary. The wines are commonly described as the most elegant and refined in the Médoc – a mix of St-Estèphe's austerity, Pauillac's power and Margaux's elegance. Vineyards here can have the lowest yields of all the major Médoc appellations. There are eleven 1855 Cru Classés (five Second, two Third and four Fourth).

St-Julien wines are characterized by their balance and refinement. Expect aromas of cassis, violets and graphite, with a silky texture and well-integrated tannins. Grand Cru Classé estates such as Château Léoville Las Cases (widely considered one of the best estates in the whole of Bordeaux), Ducru-Beaucaillou, Gruaud Larose and Léoville Poyferré sit at the top of the appellation in terms of consistent quality, complexity and finesse. Prices for these wines can be high, reflecting their prestige. Less revered but producing exceptional wines are Léoville Barton, Branaire-Ducru and the popular Beychevelle. Large estates over 100 hectares, Talbot and Lagrange, also produce very good quality and value wines as well as great white AOC Bordeaux wines.

Margaux

The southernmost appellation in the Médoc has one of the largest areas under vine. The very varied terroirs – six different types of gravel soils, limestone, chalk, clay and sand – are reflected in different styles of Margaux wines. Elegant, perfumed and complex, Margaux wines are often described as 'pretty'; they're considered rather more refined than much of the Médoc.

'Third Growth Palmer, with its great terroir and the sure-handedness of its veteran winemaker, is of First Growth quality'

Expect notes of ripe berries, violets and exotic spices, with a silky texture and fine tannins. First Growth Château Margaux sits at the top of the appellation, alongside 21 Cru Classés in total (the most of the major appellations; Margaux is also the appellation with the most organic estates). These include five Seconds, 10 Thirds, three Fourths and two Fifth Growths. Margaux is a red wine-only appellation, although Château Margaux makes one of the oldest and most famous white wines in Bordeaux, Pavillon Blanc, from vines within the AOC.

Second Growths Brane-Cantenac, Durfort-Vivens and Rauzan-Ségla are excellent. Third Growth Palmer, with its great terroir and the sure-handedness of veteran winemaker Thomas Duroux (who was winemaker at Super-Tuscan Ornellaia before joining Palmer), is of First Growth quality, continuing to surpass its counterparts. Châteaux d'Issan and

Prieuré-Lichine are other properties that perform way above their Third and Fourth Growth status respectively.

Outside of the classification, family-owned-and-run Angludet and Siran are worth seeking out.

Médoc and Haut-Médoc

It's complicated. 'The Médoc' tends to be used to describe the entire western flank of the Gironde, from the city of Bordeaux to St-Estèphe and further north. The Médoc and Haut-Médoc appellations encompass this area, except the communes we've mentioned above, which they enfold. Despite no classified estates, the area has more than 100 Cru Bourgeois estates with pockets of excellent terroir – hard and soft limestone, sandy clay and sandy gravel more suitable for Merlot than Cabernet Sauvignon. It makes classic, rich, full-bodied Bordeaux and provides great-value, easy-drinking wines in the best years, without the need for extended ageing.

Château Potensac is a star here, with the reliable Patache d'Aux, La Tour de By, Fleur La Mothe and the lesser-known Clos Manou all excellent value-picks.

Haut-Médoc refers to the higher, or northern, part of the Médoc peninsula, but confusingly, the appellation Haut-Médoc is in the southern half of the region. It stretches 50km from near Bordeaux city to St-Seurin-de-Cadourne, just north of St-Estèphe. It's home to 25 communes which include the famous names of the Médoc: Margaux, St-Julien, Pauillac, St-Estèphe and Margaux – as well as the two smaller and less revered Moulis and Listrac (each with their own AOC).

This appellation has one Third Growth, one Fourth and three Fifth Growths; there are as many well-known Cru Bourgeois estates. It also has a high concentration of estates contributing to cooperatives. Given its size, the Haut-Médoc has a range of terroirs, producing wines that vary in style but generally exhibit ripe, rich fruit flavours, firm tannins, and a pronounced sense of place. The Haut-Médoc may not have a famous name but it has some exceptional terroirs and shouldn't be overlooked in the search for classic, structured Bordeaux wines.

The Haut-Médoc Cru Classés are La Lagune, La Tour Carnet, Belgrave, Camensac and Cantemerle. You should also look out for the following well-regarded and affordable properties: Arnauld, d'Agassac, Bernadotte, Cambon La Pelouse, Caronne Ste Gemme, Citran, Clément-Pichon, d'Hanteillan, Lanessan, Liversan, Larrivaux, Malescasse, Sénéjac, Sociando-Mallet, du Taillan.

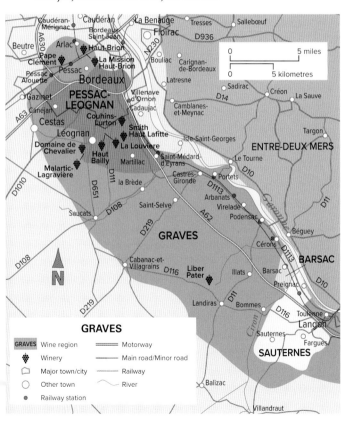

GRAVES

GRAVES Wine region		Motorway
Winery		Main road/Minor road
Major town/city		Railway
Other town		River
Railway station		

Graves and Pessac-Léognan

The Graves, named after the gravel soils that it sits on, is considered the cradle of winemaking in Bordeaux. As Jane Anson has noted, the Romans planted vines in the north of the huge region – and only to the limit of the forest clearing that they carried out around Bordeaux, or Burdigala, as they called it. Today it's the northern Graves that has the most prestige. It's the closest to Bordeaux city, and therefore the warmest part of the appellation (harvests are earlier here than elsewhere); when the first classification was drawn up in 1953, the 14 estates awarded Cru Classé status were in the north of the region. So it was that in 1987, Pessac-Léognan finally got its own sub-appellation (see Classifications page 31), with all those estates included.

The Graves used to be Bordeaux's white wine appellation (in the 1970s whites were the majority) but now two-thirds of the wines are red. The whites are considered among the best in the world; the Sauvignon Blanc-Sémillon blends of Domaine de Chevalier, Smith Haut Lafitte and Carbonnieux (to name but three) are perfumed and precise masterpieces – with prices to reflect their quality.

In the wider Graves appellation there are no classified growths, but some excellent estates; look out for Chantegrive, Clos Floridène, Cazebonne, Clos d'Uza, Crabitey and Haut Selve.

It's in the Graves that you'll find Bordeaux's most expensive and controversial wine, the £30,000-a-bottle Liber Pater. Winemaker and entrepreneur Loïc Pasquet had the idea of recreating a pre-phylloxera wine using traditional methods and indigenous grape varieties on ungrafted (i.e. not American) rootstock, and planted in high-acid, phylloxera-resistant soils. The result, he has said, is a glimpse into history; this is the style of Bordeaux they would have drunk in the 19th century.

Liber Pater isn't the only ungrafted wine in Bordeaux – Clos Manou and Château Dauzac have their own special cuvées – but it's certainly the most audacious.

Pessac-Léognan

Pessac-Léognan is renowned for both its red and white wines, which have elegance, and balanced power and refinement. Red wine aromas are typically dark fruits, tobacco and cedar, with a firm structure and long, savoury, graphite-edged finish. Often in blind tastings, if you can't immediately place the wine in a Médoc commune or St-Emilion it's probably from Pessac. Whites range from bright citrus and floral aromas to tropical and honeyed. There's often a pronounced minerality with nuances of ripe pear, peach and apricot with some honeyed notes.

The region's gravel, pebble and shingle soils mixed with clay and limestone provide excellent drainage and impart a unique mineral character to both styles of wines.

Reds tend to be quite firm and tannic when young but develop beautifully over ageing. Dry white wines here are among the best in Bordeaux, with finesse and concentration from a blend of Sémillon and Sauvignon Blanc, usually fermented and aged in French oak. They have impressive ageing abilities.

There are 16 classified estates including one First Growth (Haut-Brion – the only estate to be classified in two separate rankings, here and the 1855); and six estates make both red and white wines.

Haut-Brion's sister estate La Mission Haut-Brion would certainly be upgraded to First Growth status if the classification were to be redone today and several other estates might also expect an upgrade, emerging at the top of the Pessac quality league. These include: Smith Haut Lafitte, Haut-Bailly and the unclassified, urban winery Les Carmes Haut-Brion.

Pape Clément, Domaine de Chevalier, Malartic-Lagravière, de Fieuzal, and Carbonnieux for its white wines, are also producing excellent wines of consistent quality.

Unclassified estates worth following include La Garde, Brown, Larrivet Haut-Brion, La Louvière, Rochemorin, Lespault-Martillac and de Rouillac.

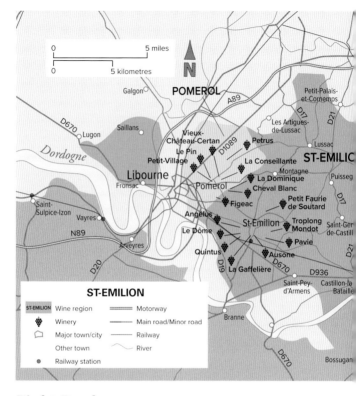

Right Bank

The Right Bank is a much larger area than the Left Bank with the two most famous appellations St-Emilion and Pomerol bordered by large swathes of land that make entry-level Bordeaux wines. Typically these wines are known for their elegance and approachability often with ripe, red fruit flavours and soft tannins thanks to cooler, more moist soils and Merlot-dominant blends. Those made on St-Emilion's limestone plateau have distinct mineral flavours and those from Pomerol's clay-rich soils can be

opulent, powerful and sensual. There are also wines made in satellite appellations and the 'côtes' which can make slightly rustic wines, but in hot vintages tend to produce lovely wines that offer unbeatable value to consumers.

St-Emilion

St-Emilion is one of the largest and least-uniform wine producing regions in Bordeaux, a huge area of land from Libourne towards the Dordogne Valley, centred on the medieval village of St-Emilion itself.

The classification is complicated. At the top is Premier Grand Cru Classé, with two levels: 'A' (two estates, Figeac and Pavie) and 'B' (not really used now); and Grand Cru Classé estates (currently 71). Below that are non-classified St-Emilion estates.

There are three distinct terroirs in St-Emilion: the renowned limestone plateau, the deep clay slopes closest to the plateau, and the flat lands below, on sandy clay. There are also areas of gravel which can be found near the border to Pomerol.

With a majority of Merlot in most blends, as well as varying degrees of Cabernet Franc, the wines can range from light and fruity, elegant and finessed to rich and complex with red fruit flavours, salinity and fresh acidity. Vines on St-Emilion's famous limestone soils benefit from excellent drainage and impart a distinctive mineral, 'wet-stone' character to the wines – it's often described as slatey, graphite or pencil-lead. Gravel soils impart elegance and aromatic complexity while those on clay can be powerful but rustic in their youth; sandy soils tend to produce wines that don't age as well as the others.

In general, St-Emilion wines are known for their lush fruit, supple tannins and elegant structure. Expect flavours of ripe berries, liquorice and chocolate, with a velvety texture and long, smooth finish.

It's here you'll find the châteaux such as Cheval Blanc and Ausone, Angelus, Pavie and Figeac. These are some of the most renowned wines in Bordeaux – and made in much smaller quantities than many classified estates on the Left Bank.

Also worth searching out are Beau-Séjour Bécot, Beauséjour (formerly Beauséjour Duffau-Lagarrosse), Bélair-Monange, Canon, Canon La Gaffelière, Larcis Ducasse, Pavie Macquin, Troplong Mondot, TrotteVieille, Valandraud, Clos Fourtet and La Mondotte.

The St-Emilion 'satellites' are smaller areas adjacent to the main appellation that also carry its name: St-Georges-St-Emilion, Montagne-St-Emilion, Lussac-St-Emilion and Puisseguin-St-Emilion. These areas tend to ripen a little later than in St-Emilion. They can sometimes be rather rustic and austere but the top wines here can often be better than wines made from vineyards on the sandier parts of St-Emilion. Because the land prices here are dramatically lower than St-Emilion, so are the prices per bottle. They remain excellent places to find small, family-owned properties often following sustainable and/or organic farming practices: Clos de Boüard, Clarisse, La Fleur Plaisance, Soleil and Vieux Château Saint André.

Pomerol

Pomerol is the smallest of all Bordeaux's major appellations, producing some of the most rare, collectible and highly prized wines in the world. It's worth a visit, but don't expect grandiose châteaux or elaborate tasting rooms – land holdings are small for the 130-odd producers (Pomerol is just over 6km in size) and very few are open to the public.

The best terroir is located on the flat plateau which contains pockets of the famous blue clay of Pomerol (where the vineyards of Pétrus are located), different depths of red clay, gravels and iron deposits. The soils become more sandy the further you go from the plateau.

Merlot thrives in Pomerol's clay and gravel soils, ripening and developing polished tannins and rich flavours. Pomerol wines are known for black cherry, plum, blackberry; you might find hints of strawberry and raspberry, with chocolate, coffee and liquorice.

This is some of the most expensive vineland in the world: around €2 million per hectare (only Pauillac is more expensive). But it's all rather academic: Pétrus (11.4 hectares) was valued at €1 billion in 2018, when a US-Colombian billionaire took a 20% stake. That would make the per-hectare value around €885 million.

Top names include: Pétrus, Le Pin, Lafleur, Trotanoy, La Conseillante, L'Eglise Clinet, L'Evangile and Vieux Château Certan.

Also excellent estates making 'relatively' good value wines are: La Fleur-Pétrus, Clos du Clocher, Guillot-Clauzel, Clinet, Hosanna, Latour à Pomerol, Petit-Village, La Pointe, Rouget and Vray Croix de Gay.

Lalande-de-Pomerol

Lalande-de-Pomerol doesn't have anything like the profile of its near-namesake. Nevertheless the appellation can produce some powerful Merlot-dominant wines. Look out for La Fleur de Boüard, Grand Ormeau, La Sergue, Domaine des Sabines and Siaurac.

Sauternes and Barsac

Sauternes and Barsac produce some of the world's finest sweet wines, renowned for their richness, acidity, complexity and ageing potential. In the right conditions – morning mists and sunny afternoons, botrytis or 'noble rot'

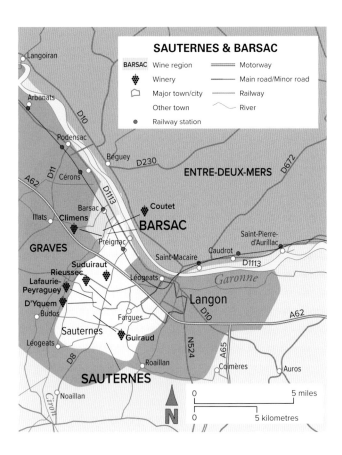

sucks the moisture from white grapes, leaving a thimbleful of intensely sweet, concentrated juice.

The region is made up of five communes including Sauternes, Barsac – the only one other than Sauternes allowed to use its own name on labels – Bommes, Fargues and Preignac. The first two make two-thirds of Bordeaux's sweet wines.

These wines are remarkably rich and sweet, with a luscious, unctuous texture and vibrant acidity. Dried fruit, tropical fruit (pineapple and mango), honey, caramel and butterscotch can meld with marmalade and gingerbread and a cornucopia of other flavours which intensify and deepen with age.

Despite their sweetness, these wines maintain a vibrant acidity that provides balance and prevents them from being cloying. This acidity also contributes to their remarkable longevity. Sauternes is capable of ageing gracefully for decades. As the wines age, they develop even greater complexity, with tertiary notes of nuts, spices and dried fruit.

These wines pair beautifully with rich foods; classic pairings include foie gras, blue cheeses like Roquefort, and desserts such as crème brûlée or apple tarte tatin. Château d'Yquem used to launch its latest vintage with a mighty spread of oysters. In Bordeaux they will be served as an apéritif, saving the champagne for the end; some reckon they make good cocktails.

The problem for Sauternes is that these wines require such patience, money and expertize to produce. The grapes are picked berry by berry, often with multiple passes through the vineyard; they can only be made when the vines are blessed with that magical combination of cold, misty mornings and hot afternoons. Because they are among the rarest wines in the world, they lie in cellars, forever awaiting that special occasion. One owner, when asked how their wine should be enjoyed, said, with a hint of desperation: 'Just open the bottle.'

Some estates are making dry wines as well as sweet in an effort to sell more wine. Château d'Yquem, the world's most famous sweet wine, owned by luxury goods company LVMH, makes an exceptional dry white called 'Y' d'Yquem. Other great Sauternes are: Coutet, Guiraud, Lafaurie-Peyraguey, Raymond-Lafon, Rieussec, Sigalas Rabaud, Suduiraut, de Fargues, Doisy-Daëne and Domaine de l'Alliance.

Bordeaux and Bordeaux Supérieur

More than 50% of Bordeaux wine is made under the Bordeaux and Bordeaux Supérieur appellations. This really is where you'll find the majority of entry-level Bordeaux and, as such, some great bargains in both red, rosé and white styles as well as some sweet and the sparkling Crémant de Bordeaux.

Red wine production dominates but because of the size and varied soils there isn't really one style of wine. However, expect relatively inexpensive, fresh fruity wines

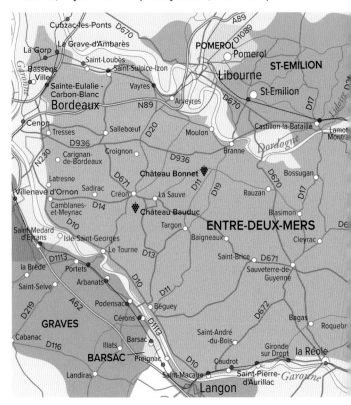

that should be drunk in their youth. Look out for the red and white Grand Village, and red Les Perrières made by parent estate Lafleur.

Entre-Deux-Mers

Entre-Deux-Mers ('between two seas') is known for its crisp, refreshing white wines made primarily from Sauvignon Blanc, Sémillon and Muscadelle. Expect aromas of citrus, green apple and fresh herbs, with a lively acidity and clean, mineral-driven finish. While this appellation may lack the prestige of some other Bordeaux regions, it offers excellent value for quality white wines. The region's clay and limestone soils provide excellent drainage and impart a distinctive mineral character to the wines, while the maritime climate ensures optimal ripening conditions, resulting in wines of bright acidity and varietal purity. Names to know include: Bauduc, de Beauregard-Ducourt, Bonnet, Sainte-Marie, Sainte-Barbe, Thieuley, Malromé and Marjosse.

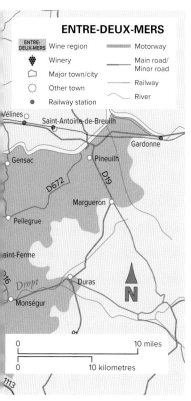

ENTRE-DEUX-MERS

ENTRE-DEUX-MERS	Wine region		Motorway
🍇	Winery		Main road/Minor road
⌂	Major town/city		Railway
○	Other town		River
●	Railway station		

Vélines
Saint-Antoine-de-Breuilh
Gardonne
Gensac
Pineuilh
D672
D19
Margueron
Pellegrue
aint-Ferme
Dropt
Duras
Monségur
N

0   10 miles
0   10 kilometres

The vines sleep under a blanket of snow at
Domaine de Chevalier, Pessac-Léognan

Lynch-Bages

The Cazes family is central to the last 100 years of Bordeaux's history. They have lived here for four generations and each has added significantly to the lustre of both their own estates and the wider region. A visit to their wonderful corner of the Médoc is highly recommended. Over the years, they have created a unique and holistic experience around Château Lynch-Bages (Pauillac Grand Cru Classé), encompassing local culture, history, shared pleasures and the inimitable French *art de vivre*.

Situated on the outskirts of Pauillac, overlooking the Gironde estuary, the Lynch-Bages vineyard (1855 Grand Cru Classé) sits on a beautiful gravelly hilltop. Formerly owned by the great Lynch family of Irish descent, the estate was acquired by the Cazes family in the late 1930s. Here, wines of international acclaim are crafted. Jane Anson, in her seminal book *Inside Bordeaux*, says that in the last decades, the Cazes family has transformed 'what was already a great wine into something quite exceptional'.

Housed in a building dating from the end of the 16th century, the historic vat room was built in the 1850s. Used until 1976, it paints a complete picture of the winemaking techniques of the period. It is still present today, miraculously intact and carefully preserved.

In 2017, the Cazes family embarked on a new chapter in the history and life of the property with the renovation of their

winemaking facilities. While in-depth analyses of the soils and vineyard have been conducted for several years, the renovation project, entrusted to the American architect Chien Chung Pei, is a natural part of this quest for excellence.

Marking four centuries of history and the culmination of four years' hard work, the 2020 vintage, the first born in the renovated cellars, opened a new chapter in the life of the estate.

Visitors are always welcome, all year long. The village of Bages is an unmissable destination for anyone visiting the Pauillac area. The renovation of this typical village of the Médoc was an enormous project for the family. Work began in 2003, house by house, and something unique has been created and has since become a meeting place for locals, winemakers and visitors. Sit at Café Lavinal, stroll around Bages' Bazaar, take a wine tasting course, buy the best local Médoc produce at the butchers, hire bicycles to meander at leisure through the Médoc countryside – the options are endless.

A stone's throw away is Château Cordeillan-Bages, a traditional *chartreuse*-style country house typical of the Médoc region, which was converted into a superb Relais & Châteaux in 1989. It has become a key destination on the Bordeaux Route des Châteaux.

Among many accolades, in 1988 *Wine Spectator* named Château Lynch-Bages Pauillac 1985 Wine of the Year. Critics are unstinting in their praise. The 2022, for example, was described by Neal Martin as 'an edifice of aromas'. In *Wine Spectator* again, James Molesworth said the 2009 – reckoned by many as one of the greatest Lynch-Bages vintages – is 'hedonistic and intellectual at the same time' and 'about as on-point as you can get'.

Content supported by Château Lynch-Bages

The grapes

Bordeaux winemakers are the master blenders of
the world, working with multiple grape varieties
from different vineyard plots to best express the
character of their terroir. And – the importance
of tradition aside – ideas of which grapes grow
best and where are constantly changing.

Château Soutard, St-Emilion

The five varieties

Bordeaux's red wine blends typically feature a combination of several grape varieties including, unsurprisingly, the two that can link their origins to France's southwest: Cabernet Sauvignon and Merlot.

Indeed, so called 'Bordeaux blends' can be found all over the world. Cabernet Sauvignon, Cabernet Franc, Merlot and often Petit Verdot and Malbec are used in Australia, Argentina, California, Chile and South Africa. Cabernet Sauvignon, the world's most widely planted grape variety, also features in Italy's Super Tuscans; the Chinese are also planting it in quantity.

Blending is both the art and signature of Bordeaux. While single-variety wines exist, growing a little in popularity as winemakers look to showcase singular expressions, they are the exception. While blending is not an obligation, some Bordeaux appellations specify in their *cahier des charges*, or rule book, a minimum and maximum percentage of certain varieties in blends.

Blends offer several advantages. They allow winemakers to deal with variable weather conditions and they create balance, complexity and terroir identities. Each grape contributes its own unique flavour – by combining grapes with different style profiles, winemakers can create more interesting and nuanced wines.

Each grape also possesses varying degrees of acidity, tannins, fruitiness and body with blends achieving a better balance overall. Like many wine regions, vintage variation plays a major role in Bordeaux, and often if one variety struggles due to adverse weather conditions, other varieties may perform better.

Blending can also enhance ageing potential, creating wines with harmonious structures that can evolve gracefully over time. More importantly, different grapes are used in blends as they are suited to Bordeaux's varied terroirs with winemakers carrying out painstaking surveys – and using generational knowledge – to determine the best location for a specific variety.

Most classified estates will begin the blending process early, in the December after harvest, finalizing it by January, giving it time to bind and meld ready for sampling during *en primeur* in April. Others prefer to keep each lot of wine ageing separately, completing the blend a few months before bottling.

The process of choosing the best barrels or lots for the blend of the first wines will invariably leave remaining batches that go towards second or even third wines, or to be sold off in bulk. These second wines are usually more approachable and affordable; they can be extremely good value in great vintages.

The white wines are blends too, mainly Sauvignon Blanc, Sémillon and Muscadelle and come in both oaked, unoaked and sweet versions.

Cabernet Sauvignon

Bordeaux's most famous (but not most widely planted grape) makes up around a fifth of total red plantings. It forms the base of the majority of wines from the Médoc and Graves. Their well-draining gravel soils, while absorbing radiating heat, provide the perfect haven for Cabernet Sauvignon to thrive, thanks to deep root systems, making vines very resistant to drought. In the best growths it can account for almost three-quarters of plantings, sometimes more.

Cabernet Sauvignon is prized for its deep colour, intense flavours and ageing potential. Full-bodied with high tannins and noticeable acidity, Cabernet has a late bud burst (one to two weeks after Merlot and Cabernet Franc), reducing susceptibility to spring frosts. Cabernet Sauvignon grapes in Bordeaux often have flavours of blackcurrant, cassis, cedar, tobacco and herbs. In cooler years, it can also show nuances of green bell peppers and mint. It can also display exceptional minerality and salinity – often in the form of liquorice, graphite and pencil lead, particularly from gravelly soils.

Merlot

Merlot dominates the red grape plantings at around 66% and is particularly prevalent in St-Emilion and Pomerol, where it's well-adapted to limestone and clay soils. It is also the majority grape in the wide swathe of land between the two rivers, the Entre-Deux-Mers, as well as the satellite appellations, the Bordeaux Côtes, where cooler and damper soils make Cabernet Sauvignon unsuitable.

Deep in colour, Merlot adds mellowness to the blend with aromas of freshly picked summer red berry fruits or fig, plum and cherry, with chocolate and toasted notes. Merlot also has floral characteristics and is often described as aromatically 'pretty'. Wines with a high proportion of Merlot can be more approachable in their youth with lush textures and supple tannins that can often soften Cabernet Sauvignon. Merlot has thinner skins and fewer tannins compared to Cabernet Sauvignon and thanks to a tendency for early bud burst can be prone to damage from frosts, coulure (when flowers fail to develop into berries resulting in reduced fruit set and potential crop loss), downy mildew (a fungus-like organism that, if left untreated, can severely damage grapevines, cause defoliation and berry rot) and botrytis (a fungus that punctures grape skins causing water evaporation and subsequent sugar concentration). Merlot can also ripen extremely quickly and as such become high in alcohol – not commonly associated with the Bordeaux identity – with winemakers having to pick at exactly the right moment to retain acidity and freshness.

Cabernet Franc

Cabernet Franc, also called Bouchet, accounts for 9.5% of red grapes in Bordeaux and is the complementary grape par excellence. In the 18th century, plantings were found throughout the Right Bank and observed to be similar to those of Cabernet Sauvignon on the Left. DNA analysis revealed that Cabernet Franc had crossed with Sauvignon Blanc to produce Cabernet Sauvignon. The two grapes remain alike although Franc buds and ripens at least a week earlier than Sauvignon and in Bordeaux acts as a certain insurance policy against cold or wet weather that may threaten the maturity of Sauvignon. Plantings are mainly on the Right Bank where it's suitable for clay-limestone soils in St-Emilion, Pomerol, Graves, Entre-Deux-Mers and the Côtes de Bordeaux. Cabernet Franc grapes produce lightly pigmented wines with pronounced perfumed aromas with violets, blackcurrants and earthy scents. It has fewer tannin than Sauvignon and tends to add smoothness and finesse to the blend.

Petit Verdot, Malbec and Carménère

Just 2% of plantings are dedicated to Petit Verdot, Malbec and Carménère. Petit Verdot suits the gravelly soils of the Left Bank and contributes deep violet colours, dark fruit and spiced aromas as well as firm tannins and high acidity. Malbec, also known as Côt, was a historically important variety in Bordeaux and, whilst rare today, is growing in popularity. It brings a rich colour and a lot of tannins with elements of leather and pepper. Carménère was one of the original grape varieties in the Médoc but was destroyed by both oidium and phylloxera in 1867 and for many years the grape was presumed to be extinct. Having found fame in Chile, there are not many Carménère vineyards in France but some Bordeaux producers are experimenting with its reintroduction in a broader trend of grape variety diversification and a way to adapt to changing climate conditions. It's known for its rich, spicy character with dark fruit, pepper and herbal touches and high acidity.

The whites

White wine production is dominated by Sémillon and
Sauvignon Blanc with 45% and 43% of total plantings
respectively. The remaining 12% comprises 5% of Muscadelle
and 7% 'others' including Ugni Blanc, Colombard, Merlot
Blanc and Sauvignon Gris. A tiny number of Chardonnay
vines, and even Riesling, are also planted (mostly
experimentally) but cannot be labelled as being from
Bordeaux or anywhere within the region.

Sémillon

Sémillon, valued for its richness and roundness, is used
for Bordeaux's dry and sweet white wines. The majority of
plantings are in Sauternes and Barsac, where the grape has
a tendency to develop *botrytis cinerea* (noble rot), resulting
in lusciously sweet wines. It has almost no presence in
the Médoc. As a minor blending partner to Sauvignon
Blanc it can add ripe stone fruit aromas of peach, apricot
and nectarine as well as flavours of tropical fruit such as
pineapple and mango.

Sauvignon Blanc

According to historical sources, Sauvignon Blanc originated in Bordeaux, or its broader region. In southwest France it grew vigorously and wild – hence the 'sauvage' root of its name. It has been cultivated in Bordeaux for centuries and is still found all over the region today. It can be used as a minor blending partner for sweet wines and increasingly for dry whites, often unblended. The grape buds late but ripens early, allowing it to perform in maritime climates where it can develop a balance between acidity and sugar levels. It has crisp acidity, citrus fruit flavours and herbaceous aromas and is especially prevalent in the wines from the Entre-Deux-Mers, Graves and Pessac-Léognan, although it is the principal grape of Château Margaux's Pavillon Blanc.

Muscadelle

Muscadelle is a minor grape variety in white Bordeaux blends valued for its aromatic intensity and floral notes, such as orange blossom, jasmine and honeysuckle. It adds fragrance, elegance and a touch of sweetness which enhances its complexity and charm.

Sauvignon Gris

Sauvignon Gris, a mutation of Sauvignon Blanc with slightly pink-grey berries, has typically lower acidity than its parent variety. While not as widely planted or well known as Sauvignon Blanc, it is cultivated in Bordeaux particularly in the Entre-Deux-Mers. Ugni Blanc and Colombard are minority grapes with few plantings across the region.

Developments

With changing weather patterns, better viticultural practices and new consumer trends, Bordeaux is seeing a slow revolution in grape plantings. These include replanting different but traditional varieties on more suitable soils (replacing Merlot with Cabernet Sauvignon for instance), propagating existing vines that demonstrate desirable qualities onto rootstocks to create new vines (known as massal selection) or experimenting with new grapes entirely.

The first two methods are time-consuming, with areas of uprooted vines needing at least a few years' rest before they can be planted again, while massal selection involves the identification and subsequent monitoring of superior vines based on grape quality, yield, disease resistance and adaptability to terroir and climate. Cuttings of these 'mother vines' are then taken and grafted onto new rootstocks preserving the unique characteristics of the vineyards. Massal selection can help mitigate the risks of vineyard diseases and pests by promoting diversity and resistance within the vine population.

Bordeaux leverages generations of knowhow regarding vine suitability, with a constant push for improvement, all while respecting history and tradition. In prestigious appellations where quality and tradition are paramount, it is not uncommon to find vineyards with a significant proportion of older vines, some of which may be 30 years old or more, and prized for their deeper root systems, lower yields and greater concentration of flavour. Some vineyards – notably TrotteVieille in St-Emilion and Mouton Rothschild in Pauillac, have centuries-old vines still in production.

Many estates have rigorous replanting systems in place to maintain a constant production. Less lucrative appellations may have higher densities of young vines as growers establish new vineyards. It came as quite a surprise when in 2021 France's national appellation body, the INAO, officially approved six new grape varieties to help Bordeaux wine producers adapt to climate change. The four new red varieties include Touriga Nacional, Marselan, Castets and Arinarnoa, the whites Alvarinho and Liliorila.

Currently only the Bordeaux and Bordeaux Supérieur appellations have applied for planting rights to see how the grapes respond to warmer and drier summers. Appellation rules state growers are limited to planting just 5% of their vineyards with these varieties and which must not exceed 10% of the final blend for each colour.

Bernard Magrez, a prominent Bordeaux wine producer and owner of four classified estates, has also been involved in initiatives aimed at addressing the challenges posed by climate change. In 2013 an experimental vineyard was established at La Tour Carnet, the Médoc's largest wine estate, to explore innovative vineyard management techniques. Over 80 different grape varieties were planted to see which could be used to retain the taste and flavour profile of Bordeaux's great wines while adapting to warmer temperatures, changing rainfall patterns and increased weather variability. The team are at the forefront of efforts to future-proof Bordeaux vineyards in the face of uncertainties. The first grapes were harvested in 2022 with results for the best grapes and processes going forward still outstanding.

How to read a Bordeaux label

The great Bordeaux estates aren't worried about standing out on a supermarket shelf, but still they put endless thought into the merest tweak of their label. Some go for the ultra-minimal look, some opt for classic;

David Hockney – since 1945, Mouton has commissioned an important artist for the label. The roll call includes Henry Moore, Miró, Chagall, Picasso, Andy Warhol, Dalí, Lucian Freud, Jeff Koons, the then Prince Charles...

Toute la récolte a été mise en bouteilles au Château – the entire vintage was bottled at the château. Before the advent of mass-produced glass bottles in the 1820s, all wine was shipped in barrels and bottled by wine merchants, but it wasn't until the 20th century that bottling at the château became commonplace. Starting with the 1924 vintage, Mouton was the first estate to bottle all its wine in situ; stating this on the label was a guarantee of its quality and provenance

2014 – the vintage: the year the grapes were harvested

Château Mouton Rothschild – the name of the property. Nathaniel de Rothschild re-christened Château Brane-Mouton when he bought it in 1853

Appellation Pauillac Contrôlée – note that Mouton does not add 1er Grand Cru Classé en 1855 to make clear it's a First Growth. Anyone picking up a bottle of Mouton should be expected to understand its rank

Baronne Philippine de Rothschild – the much-loved matriarch who died in 2014, Philippine de Rothschild survived the Holocaust (in which her mother died) and became an actress of some acclaim before inheriting Mouton in 1988, the first woman in five generations to lead the family business

in Bordeaux you will seldom, if ever, find a simple statement of the grape varieties in the blend. Many readers will be familiar with terms such as 'Cru Classé en 1855'; others might want a note of explanation...

Domaine de Chevalier – the name of the property

2000 – the vintage: the year the grapes were harvested

Mis en bouteille au château – signifies that the wine was produced and bottled at the property. See note for Mouton, left

Olivier Bernard – when the Bernard family of wine merchants bought Domaine de Chevalier in 1983, Olivier's father asked him to run it. He was 23; since then he has transformed it into one of the leaders of Pessac-Léognan and one of the most renowned estates in Bordeaux

Grand Cru Classé de Graves – the wine is classified under the Graves classification of 1953 (see Bordeaux's classification systems explained page 31)

Pessac-Léognan, Appellation Pessac-Léognan Contrôlée – appellation within the Graves, introduced in 1987 to distinguish its finest red and white wines, all of them in the northern part of the region

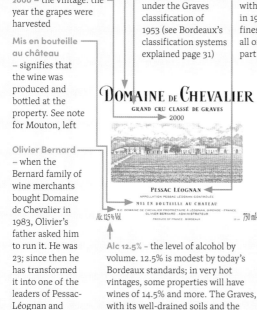

DOMAINE DE CHEVALIER
GRAND CRU CLASSÉ DE GRAVES
2000

PESSAC LÉOGNAN
APPELLATION PESSAC LÉOGNAN CONTROLÉE
MIS EN BOUTEILLE AU CHATEAU
S.C. DOMAINE DE CHEVALIER PROPRIÉTAIRE À LÉOGNAN, GIRONDE - FRANCE
OLIVIER BERNARD - ADMINISTRATEUR
PRODUCE OF FRANCE - BORDEAUX

Alc 12.5% Vol.   750 ml

750ml – there are many wonderful theories as to how this (and not a full litre) came to be the European standard for wine (750ml is the capacity of the average glass-blower's lungs, for example). The truth is prosaic: wine was shipped in 225-litre barrels and wine merchants (who did the bottling) came up with the roundest way of breaking down that quantity: a barrel held 300 bottles of 750ml each

Alc 12.5% – the level of alcohol by volume. 12.5% is modest by today's Bordeaux standards; in very hot vintages, some properties will have wines of 14.5% and more. The Graves, with its well-drained soils and the cooling effect of the Garonne River, produces wines of great finesse, although 13.5–14% is more usual here

Visiting Bordeaux

The seasons, the *fêtes* and *Portes Ouvertes*

For many, the best months to visit Bordeaux are May to September. The weather is at its peak, it's perfect for outdoor living and beach breaks, and there are dozens of fêtes du village, markets and festivals.

A tasting at Fête le Vin

Spring, for a visiting northern European, is a delightful time, with April temperatures climbing into the high 20s.

Summers can be ferociously hot – great for swimming in the sea and exploring the coast (don't miss the magnificent Dune du Pilat, Europe's largest sand dune). August is a very quiet time in the vineyards, with almost everyone on holiday for the entire month.

Autumn is wonderful if you want to catch the vines in their majesty, just before harvest; October can be deliciously warm – a great time to explore the city. Harvest starts at the end of August; for two months vineyards bustle with activity as grapes are picked and winemaking begins.

Winter in Bordeaux can be magical, especially when the vineyards are covered in frost. Temperatures seldom go below freezing, and days can be mild – around 10°C is average in December. It's also outside the tourist season so it's easier to book restaurants.

Tasting the wines and visiting châteaux

For some, it's enough to press their face against the hallowed gates of Château Margaux; others prefer a visit and a tasting in one of the hundreds of estates that are open to the public (see Châteaux tours and tastings pages 118–137).

If your time is limited then you might consider one of the huge tasting events put on by bodies such as the Union des Grands Crus de Bordeaux (see below).

Le Weekend des Grands Crus de Bordeaux (ugcb.net), in June, is held inside a large hangar on the quay. This is a good chance to taste some of the best wines and classified growths, and meet the people who make them.

Fête le Vin (bordeaux-wine-festival.com), in June, is Bordeaux's summer fête. It's held all along the Bordeaux quays, with wine tastings, local cuisine, workshops, river cruises and masterclasses led by renowned winemakers. One of the unmissable sights of the Fête is the traditional procession of half a dozen tall ships up the river

Portes Ouvertes (Open Door) weekends. From April to December at least one of the 60 appellations will have *Portes Ouvertes* days, with the majority in spring and summer. They're an excellent opportunity to see châteaux, meet winemakers and taste dozens of wines. They can be grand or more villagey affairs but there's always a festival atmosphere (at the Côtes de Bourg weekend they party till 2am); many offer bike hire and mini trains to get you around the châteaux. If no website is listed try websites like bordeaux-tourism.co.uk for details and exact dates.

Blaye spring wine festival: April (www.vin-blaye.com)
Médoc: April (www.portesouvertesenmedoc.com)
Lalande-de-Pomerol: April
St-Emilion: May (www.vins-saint-emilion.com)
Côtes de Bourg: May (www.cotes-de-bourg.com/portes-ouvertes)
Cadillac Côtes de Bordeaux: end May/early June
(www. cadillaccotesdebordeaux.com/)
Entre-Deux-Mers: June (www.entredeuxmers.com)
Castillon Côtes de Bordeaux: September (www.tourisme-castillonpujols.fr)
Graves: October (www.nouvelle-aquitaine-tourisme.com)
Fronsac: October (www.tourisme-fronsadais.com)
Pomerol: October (www.vins-pomerol.fr)
Sauternes: June and November
Pessac-Léognan: December

Fête le Vin

How to visit a First Growth

Two of the five First Growths, and other of the great names, welcome visitors – up to a point. Don't ever expect to just turn up at the gates and ring the bell. You won't be let in.

Château Mouton Rothschild and Château Margaux are among the most prestigious estates you can actually visit in the Médoc. On the Right Bank, Château Pavie and Figeac, both St-Emilion Premier Grand Cru Classé A, are open to visitors although appointments are essential. At Mouton – where there is a gallery of the original label art – you need to book at least two months in advance. Latour does not admit visitors.

Château Margaux opens its doors for tours of its impressive cellars, although tastings are reserved for professionals. Even if you're not a pro, the chance to park and snap that iconic photo of Château Margaux through its gates makes the visit worthwhile for some. Sauternes First Growth Château d'Yquem also offers tours and tastings.

Booking your visit is a matter of planning ahead and persistence. For the most part, you'll need to email at least two months in advance. When you do get an appointment, never be late. Some châteaux are known to make exceptions for collectors or enthusiasts (it helps to have an introduction from a wine merchant). Lafite and Haut-Brion are under renovation so try their sister properties (Château Duhart-Milon in Pauillac or La Mission Haut-Brion in Pessac).

Some estates are simply off-limits, no matter how determined you are. Pétrus and Le Pin are personal invitation-only. Cheval Blanc is similarly private, and Ausone isn't even signposted

For many more estates to visit see Châteaux tours and tastings (pages 118–136)

And the rest...

Bordeaux offers much more than vineyards and tastings. Be sure to explore some of the area's other cultural attractions, including:

- The Bordeaux Wine Museum – 'La Cité du Vin': discover the fascinating history of Bordeaux wine through interactive exhibits, multimedia displays and tastings.
- The CAPC Museum of Contemporary Art: housed in a former warehouse, this avant-garde museum specializes in international contemporary art.
- Bordeaux Cathedral – Cathédrale Saint-André: a stunning Gothic landmark, with intricate carvings and towering spires.
- The D2 Wine Route: the 'Route des Châteaux', where you'll pass some of Bordeaux's most prestigious estates (see Wine routes page 102).
- Quartier des Chartrons: Bordeaux's former wine merchant district, where elegant mansions, antique shops and art galleries line the cobbled streets.
- Sunday morning market at Marché des Capucins: fresh produce, gourmet delicacies, antiques and bric-a-brac.
- La Grosse Cloche: Bordeaux's medieval bell tower – one of the oldest belfries in France, which served as part of the city's defensive fortifications in the Middle Ages – has panoramic views of the city.
- Jardin Public: manicured lawns and shaded walkways; the botanical garden keeps a huge collection of plants from around the world.

Château Ferrière, Margaux

Pessac-Léognan – The Garden of Bordeaux

Pessac-Léognan is both the youngest and one of the oldest of Bordeaux's appellations. It was created in 1987 – but vines have been grown here for more than 2,000 years. This ancient terroir, home to 14 Grand Cru Classés, including the legendary Château Haut-Brion, is also less than half an hour from the city of Bordeaux. It's incredibly easy to get to by car, tram, bike or boat, so it's *the* perfect destination for a day trip.

The Garden of Bordeaux

'I want to listen to my land and understand it. I'm searching for the ideal balance between the soils, the plants, those who work here and make the wine, those who live nearby and all those who drink it; this is why my wine is true.' The words of one vigneron sum up the spirit of the region; we put the environment at the forefront of everything we do.

This is a large part of the beauty of the region. It's an oasis of green, with famous vineyards, beautiful country walks, forest trails and waterways; a region of Grand Cru Classés, family estates, historic châteaux and medieval fortresses. Whether you're a wine lover or a nature lover, you'll find dozens of activities, from tasting sessions to outstanding gastronomy and first-class accommodation.

This is the quintessentially local 'Esprit de Bordeaux', and it's everywhere, from the innovation of precision viticulture to the families who continue to farm their land, as they have done for generations.

The true taste of Bordeaux

Pessac-Léognan is the only high-end appellation of Bordeaux producing reds and whites with classified growth in both colours.

The dry white wines, blends of Sémillon and Sauvignon Blanc (often with a touch of Muscadelle for its delicate floral aromas), are acclaimed by wine lovers and collectors alike for their structure and luscious fruit.

The reds are internationally renowned: Cabernet Sauvignon, with its mineral notes typical of the appellation, has structure, power, harmony, consistency and longevity. Merlot adds suppleness, and other varieties – Cabernet Franc, Petit Verdot, Malbec and Carménère – can also be used to complement the finesse, silky tannins, rich aromatic bouquet and longevity for which Bordeaux's red wines are renowned.

We are proud to uphold the values of the purest Bordeaux style, harnessing its ideal of restraint, balance and authenticity, while always striving to innovate. As one connoisseur noted: 'Pessac-Léognan wines are the true taste of Bordeaux.'

Content supported by the Syndicat Viticole de Pessac-Léognan

The towns and villages

It might be the most sophisticated wine region in the world, but Bordeaux – when you get beyond the pull of the city – is truly rural. Many a visitor to the Médoc is stumped by the lack of watering-places. The following is a brief guide to where to go and what to see in the communes.

Château Cos d'Estournel

St-Estèphe

At around 1 hour 10 minutes by car from Bordeaux city, a drive up to St-Estèphe is really only worth it if you're an outdoor enthusiast and want to explore the appellation's famous châteaux with stunning views of vines with the Gironde estuary as a backdrop. Beyond Cos d'Estournel's La Maison d'Estournel, a fabulous hotel and restaurant (with an 18-metre heated pool and electric bikes to hire), there are limited dining and accommodation options so pack a picnic before you go.

The best way to experience St-Estèphe is by bike with a 15km circular route that takes roughly two hours from start to finish (it can also be driven). The journey will take you from the Romanesque St-Etienne church and Maison du Vin in the village past more than 17 different estates including Calon Ségur, Montrose and Cos d'Estournel with its incredible exotic architecture.

If you're after a tasting and tour, Phélan Ségur, La Haye, Laffitte Carcasset, de Côme and Tronquoy Lalande all welcome visitors.

The drive may be long but it's also incredibly scenic and will take you up the famous D2 Route des Châteaux past many a picture perfect moment. Boating, fishing or bird watching enthusiasts will also enjoy the charms of St-Estèphe and its neighbouring town of Pauillac.

Pauillac

The small town of Pauillac lies at the centre of the appellation which hugs the Gironde estuary. It's surprisingly small and somewhat run-down considering it's home to three of the most famous wine estates in the world. The town consists of a few docks at the water's edge and a broad boulevard with a number of cafés, bakeries and restaurants dotted along it. There's a weekly Saturday market, and the Médoc's largest Maison du Tourisme et du Vin, with detailed information on all things *médocain* and a wide choice of wines and local foods

Pauillac town is also the start and finishing point of the annual Marathon du Médoc. This takes place every September and combines a full marathon with wine tasting. The atmosphere is unlike any other marathon you might have taken part in. The 26.2-mile race typically features 20 stops as runners pass through the vineyards, villages and château grounds of the Médoc. Participants can pause to enjoy a glass of wine – the first sip after a few kilometres – as well as indulge in gourmet foods and refuel with specialities such as oysters, cheese and ice cream. Entries usually open on March 1st and with only 8,500 places they sell out quickly.

But really if you're coming to Pauillac, you're coming for First Growths, scenic shots of fairytale château buildings and great tours and tastings. Lafite and Latour are notoriously difficult to visit – they're usually reserved for professionals with any other visits down to the discretion of their teams. It's worth asking directly or going through a reputable guide if this is a must on your visit. You can still take pictures of Lafite's gorgeous grounds and historic building from the road. Mouton however is open during the week, with two-and-a-half hour tours covering the art of winemaking, the wine museum and art gallery, and a private tasting.

You can also book a visit to Pichon Baron with its new tasting room and sun terrace, Pontet-Canet, Pichon Longueville Comtesse de Lalande, Pedesclaux, Haut-Bages Libéral, Duhart-Milon and Clerc Milon.

For other châteaux to visit, dine at or stay the night in, see Châteaux tours and tastings pages 118–137.

St-Julien

Visitors to St-Julien come to marvel at the splendour of the château buildings and to take part in tours and tastings. There isn't much more to see in the small town with a population of fewer than 800 people. It may not be as tightly packed with vineyards and châteaux as the other towns but it does have a large number of wineries varying in price and quality – and there are some great experiences to be had here with visits possible at many estates: Gruaud Larose, Léoville Barton, Lagrange, Branaire-Ducru, Beychevelle, Léoville Poyferré and Talbot. The non-classified Teynac, La Bridane and de Lauga also offer tourism experiences.

Margaux

Margaux isn't big but it's packed with winery action. It's about 40 minutes by train from Bordeaux Gare St-Jean, and plenty of estates are within walking distance from the station. In fact, there's an 8.5km circular walking or cycling route that takes you past 18 estates including Lascombes, Issan, Margaux, Palmer and Rauzan-Ségla. Châteaux Ferrière, Labegorce, Kirwan, Brane Cantenac, Cantenac Brown and d'Arsac are also open for tours and tastings. There are numerous lunch options: the fabulous contemporary restaurant at Marquis de Terme; the convivial Marquis d'Alesme Becker's La Table de Nathalie, or a pizzeria called L'Indigo (on the fast road south out of Margaux) that's a good place for a refreshing beer after a tasting. Accommodation options include beautiful rooms at Giscours (the only estate with a full-size cricket pitch) or du Tertre and Marojallia (both of which have swimming pools). You can get tourist information at the Maison du Vin du Tourisme, and there's an excellent wine shop, Cave d'Ulysse. To complete your day, stop off at the chocolate factory Mademoiselle de Margaux for some of their famous Sarments du Médoc - chocolate twigs resembling bundles of vine cuttings – and Perles du Médoc, chocolate covered white grapes.

Château La Louvière

Pessac-Léognan

Pessac-Léognan, a short tram-ride from the centre of Bordeaux, is a wine lover's paradise, a gentle region of undulating hills and small towns, dotted with world-famous châteaux. This appellation is known for producing some of the finest red and white wines in Bordeaux (home to all of the Graves appellation's most famous wines), offering visitors a rich tapestry of viticulture, gastronomy and local culture.

The wines may not be as familiar as those from the Médoc but they can be equally as delicious, particularly if you're a fan of white wines as many of the best in the region are made here. The appellation comprises 10 smaller villages, the primary two of which are the titular Pessac and Léognan.

Pessac

Pessac is easily accessible from Bordeaux city, by car, tram or bike (you can take the bike on the tram if you wish).

The centre of town is a lively mix of restaurants, cafés and food shops; on Sundays there's a huge outdoor market. There's a cycle route which takes you past the UNESCO World Heritage Site of Le Corbusier's Cité Frugès, a residential neighbourhood with geometric shapes and panoramic terraces built in the 1920s. The grand Château Pape Clément, whose vines were planted at the request of the Archbishop of Bordeaux, the future Pope Clement V, runs tastings (and you can stay in one of its luxurious bedrooms). There's an 18th-century water mill, Moulin de Noes (a great place for a picnic). The nearby Bourgailh Forest has a walking trail, a vast tropical greenhouse, a skateboard park, an open-air amphitheatre, an observatory and a zoo.

Léognan

Viticulture, gastronomy and local culture come together in Léognan, a typical French town with bakeries, hairdressers, butchers, supermarkets, a post office and schools. Don't miss the Romanesque church of Saint-Martin de Léognan, which was a chapel on the pilgrim trail to Santiago de Compostela in Spain in the 11th century. Château La Louvière is notable for its 18th-century architecture, inspired by the work of the Parisian architect Victor Louis, who built Bordeaux's splendid Grand Théâtre. There's a bustling Saturday market, an excellent place to experience the local flavours and ambiance. Léognan has some of the grandest châteaux, from First Growth Château Haut-Brion, Pape Clément and Les Carmes Haut-Brion; Smith Haut Lafitte, renowned for both its red and white wines, has the luxurious Les Sources de Caudalie spa; owners Florence and Daniel Cathiard are also art collectors, filling the vineyards with sculptures, like the magnificent Barry Flanagan hare that has become the emblem of the estate.

Malartic-Lagravière, de Fieuzal, Haut-Bailly, Carbonnieux and Domaine de Chevalier are all in the commune of Léognan. All of the above, with the exception of Les Carmes, are among the Cru Classés de Graves.

And they are all open for visits (you'll have to book Haut-Brion months in advance).

St-Emilion

This lovely town, which in 1999 became the first wine region to be listed as a UNESCO World Heritage Site, has a long and venerable history; its monastic past is visible in every cobbled street, ancient alleyway and historic building. It is said to be named after the 8th-century monk Emilion, who lived as a hermit in a cave carved into the limestone rock, where he performed acts of healing and kindness for the local population. As his reputation grew, the monastic community which formed around his cave eventually became the town of St-Emilion. Various religious groups including Benedictine, Augustinian and Dominican monks lived in the town and built the monuments still standing today.

The town itself is full of wine merchants, each with its own specialism, from large format bottles to mature vintages. Almost all run regular tastings. Unsurprisingly you may not find many wines made outside of Bordeaux here, but you will find some atypical sparkling wines made in St-Emilion itself. A former monastery, the Cloître des Cordeliers offers tours and tastings. Their standard non-vintage sparkling is excellent.

Dining options (see Where to eat and drink in St-Emilion pages 167–172) include L'Envers du Décor as well as the upmarket Michelin-starred La Table de Pavie and Logis de la Cadène. On your way out of the town, stop by the Maison du Vin for a large selection of local wines at great prices, and macarons – a local speciality dating back to the early 1600s.

Outside town is the Michelin-starred Les Belles Perdrix at Troplong Mondot. A more modest option is Le Jardin restaurant at Château Petit Faurie de Soutard which has a terrace and balcony overlooking the vines. Château La Dominique's Terrasse Rouge has a lively brasserie-type atmosphere with panoramic views over St-Emilion and Pomerol. Château de Candale's L'Atelier de Candale also has incredible views with a lovely outdoor terrace in the summer.

Accommodation-wise, choose from one of the gorgeous offerings at Troplong Mondot including the house in the vines, a two-bed cottage with an open fire in the winter, and terrace overlooking St-Emilion with incredible sunsets in the summer. Bellefont-Belcier has a guesthouse in a tranquil countryside setting; there's the luxury, five-star Grand Barrail hotel. In nearby St-Christophe-des-Bardes, the luxurious villa Maison Dubreuil is available for rent.

With so many beautifully restored châteaux buildings, impressive cellars and excellent tourism attractions, St-Emilion definitely offers the greatest choice in terms of tours and tasting opportunities, most of them reasonably priced. These include Rol Valentin, Soutard, Fleur Cardinale, Montlabert, de Ferrand, Mauvinon, Fonplegade, La Dominique, Guibeau, de Pressac, La Croizille, Cadet Bon and Villemaurine.

St-Emilion

Pomerol

Pomerol, for wine lovers, is a name as potent as any, but it's a drab little town offering little beyond a church, a school and a wine shop that never seems to be open. There's no boulangerie or bar but there is a lovely restaurant called La Table de Catusseau, frequented by winemakers and vineyard workers. The busiest location is usually just outside the gates of Pétrus where cars line up for photo opps. Many properties are tiny and family-owned. Estates that are open to the public by appointment include: Beauregard, Bonalgue, Gazin, Taillefer, Clinet, Petit-Village, Mazeyres and de Sales.

Sauternes & Barsac

The two communes of Sauternes and Barsac are the source of some of the world's greatest sweet wines, home to the greatest number of 1855 classified growths, yet the second smallest appellation in Bordeaux. They offer an enchanting getaway from the city where morning mists swirl around ancient vines and medieval château buildings, almost all of which are family-run.

Château d'Yquem, Sauternes

Sauternes has been leading the way in oenotourism for some time and is full of innovative tours, tastings and activities. The *Portes Ouvertes* weekend (usually in November) and Sauternes Fête le Vin (usually in June) are two very popular events.

Public transport options are limited here so you'll need a car. The nearest train station is Langon, about 40 minutes from Bordeaux. The small village of Sauternes itself is beautifully looked-after with stone houses and rows of vines climbing the slopes. In the centre is the 17th-century Saint-Pierre-ès-Liens church, a wine shop and the Maison du Sauternes where you can sample and purchase 55 different wines as well as purchase local delicacies such as foie gras or Sauternes grape jelly. Barsac also has a Maison du Vin.

'Château Guiraud has a tasting with caviar, electric bikes and a lovely restaurant'

Estates worth visiting include the five-star Château Lafaurie-Peyraguey, parts of which date back to the 13th century, and its two-Michelin-starred Lalique restaurant. It's next door to the greatest name in Sauternes, Château d'Yquem, which offers a range of tours and tastings.

Other estates open to the public include Château Guiraud (including a tasting with caviar, electric bikes and a lovely restaurant called Le Cercle Guiraud), and Rayne Vigneau, which has a blending workshop, an escape game, a treetop tasting and a trip around Sauternes.

Sigalas Rabaud has five guest rooms within its 17th-century family-owned *chartreuse*. Château La Tour Blanche has a pop-up tapas bar as well as wine and cheese pairings, a workshop on bats and tours of the estate. Guiraud runs bike tours and Lafaurie-Peyraguey has a 'must-see gastronomic stopover' with a 2,600-strong wine list.

Entre-Deux-Mers

The Entre-Deux-Mers, between the Garonne and Dordogne rivers, is a picturesque wine-producing region with nine different appellations and 133 communes. It's a richly diverse area and home to all wine styles including red, rosé, dry and sweet white and sparkling wines (Crémant de Bordeaux).

The area's winemaking history goes back to the Romans. It's eclipsed by the starrier appellations, but it's a lovely part of Bordeaux, with wooded lanes leading to *petits châteaux* and unpretentious villages. It's also Bordeaux's largest winemaking area, where the majority of estates are family-run, offering informal visits, accommodation and affordable wines. From B&Bs and wellness retreats to restored *pigeonniers* and gigantic wine barrels, there's everything from quirky to luxury, with plenty of family-friendly choices.

Indeed, Entre-Deux-Mers is a great choice for a family holiday. Wine is the draw but the region is filled with incredible architecture, great restaurants, a commitment to preserving biodiversity and UNESCO World Heritage Sites like Sauve-Majeure Abbey; there are cycle tracks, surfing and waterskiing spots and dancing pop-ups throughout the summer.

Among the rolling hills and sunflower fields, you'll find large estates, fortified villages with bustling medieval market squares and church steeples dotting the landscape.

Langoiran has its religious monuments and castle ruins; Cadillac also has a castle, ramparts and wine museum; Sainte-Croix-du-Mont (where they also make sweet wine) is a pretty village with great views; Pondaurat has an 11km-loop walk around two remarkable churches; the ancient medieval city of La Réole has a monastery abbey, stunning church, towers and ramparts as well as an excellent Saturday morning market (one of the best in the area).

The charming little town of Monségur has ramparts, a cute square, excellent bakery and an annual jazz festival that attracts international attention. It also has a small but excellent market on Fridays. The fortified village of Castelmoron d'Albret is built on a rocky outcrop; in Sauveterre-de-Guyenne, founded in 1281, you can still see the 14th-century stone gates. Blasimon has a Benedictine abbey and a fortified water mill, while Créon has a remarkable abbey and excellent market on Wednesdays. Branne's Thursday market is worth visiting, as is its restaurant Le Caffé Cuisine, frequented by winemakers and owners. Pellegrue is also worth noting – founded in the 13th century, it has a centre square with two churches and three castles from the 13th, 15th and 18th centuries. Its weekly market is on a Wednesday.

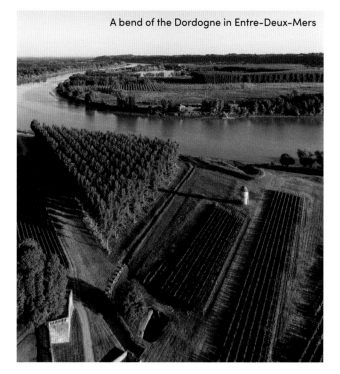

A bend of the Dordogne in Entre-Deux-Mers

Wine routes

Whether you want to take a selfie at the gates of Château Margaux or pair oysters and white wine at Arcachon, a trip to Bordeaux needs planning. Here we list a few ways to spend a day, a weekend or a week in the world's greatest wine region.

La Place du Parlement, Bordeaux

Bordeaux city is easy to get to and easy to find your way around. Mérignac airport, 12km (7.5 miles) west of the city centre, is served direct by major European cities and is less than half an hour from the centre of town by taxi, tram, shuttle bus or hire car.

The city is served by an efficient public transport system, including buses, an excellent tram service, e-bikes and scooters. Above all, Bordeaux is very walkable, especially within the historic centre, which is criss-crossed with pedestrian-friendly streets.

The tram is an excellent option for visiting **Pessac-Léognan** (see page 57), a charming suburb with a hilly, wooded feel. First Growth Château Haut-Brion is here, as well as a clutch of famous properties – Smith Haut Lafitte, Domaine de Chevalier, Malartic-Lagravière and others. Tram line A from the centre of Bordeaux takes you to within a 10-minute walk from Château Les Carmes Haut-Brion (no relation to its illustrious neighbour but a fascinating château to visit).

To get further afield, to visit the **Médoc** for example, hiring a car is the best option. There is a train (main stops are Margaux, 43 minutes from the centre, Moulis-Listrac and Pauillac, an hour away) but the châteaux are very spread out – the only way to get from St-Julien to Pauillac, for example, is by car. The D2, known as the Route des Châteaux, is the arterial road that runs through the heart of the Médoc. It's a scenic drive with stunning vineyard views and easy access to all the famous properties.

The one appellation that is relatively easy to explore by train and foot is **Margaux**. Some fine châteaux – Lascombes, Marquis de Terme, Ferrière, Durfort-Vivens and Marquis d'Alesme – are a 15-minute walk from the station; Palmer, Margaux, Rauzan-Gassies, Rauzan-Ségla and Brane-Cantenac are further away but walkable. Many properties now offer bikes with routes through the vineyards.

For **Sauternes**, there are hourly departures from Bordeaux's Gare Saint-Jean to Gare de Cérons. Château de Cérons is a 10-minute walk from the station.

St-Emilion is a 35-minute train journey from Gare Saint-Jean. Once in St-Emilion, the village and its surrounding vineyards are easily explored on foot – it's a 10–15 minute walk from the station to the centre of town (you pass Canon La Gaffelière on your way there).

Depending on how many châteaux you want to see in St-Emilion, you can either go on foot or hire an e-bike. You can easily walk to TrotteVieille or Troplong Mondot (Angelus is a bit further). To venture further – to Fleur Cardinale for example, or to explore Pomerol, you'll need to have a car, or possibly a powerful electric bike.

Cycling (and e-biking) is become more and more popular. Several companies offer picturesque guided tours along the back roads to the châteaux. Some estates (such as Troplong Mondot in St-Emilion, Léoville Poyferré in St-Julien and Suduiraut in Sauternes) have e-bikes.

Day trip 1 St-Emilion

Châteaux to visit (see The Guide page 116 for details):
Soutard
Le Dôme
de Ferrand
de Pressac
La Dominique
Fleur de Boüard

The UNESCO-listed St-Emilion is one of the most beautiful towns in France and the perfect base to explore surrounding vineyards by bike.

Start your day with a coffee and croissant at Le Médiéval before taking an e-bike or the tourist train through the old town and the vineyards. This is the best way to see the rolling hills and the great estates among the famous limestone outcrops of St-Emilion.

Visit La Dominique for a tour and tasting – and lunch at the restaurant La Terrasse Rouge (see page 142) with its panoramic views of the vineyard; Château de Pressac also has superb views.

For classic fare and a well-priced wine list, head to L'Envers du Décor (see page 171) before climbing the 53-metre bell tower of Eglise Monolithe – the 11th-century monolithic church, unique of its kind, its maze of tunnels and catacombs carved out of limestone – for a superb view.

St-Emilion has a very good selection of wine shops, for new and old vintages and for bargain hunting: Maison du Vin for a wine shop/tourist information centre with a large selection of well-priced bottles; Vignobles et Châteaux for large-format and 'recently released' bottles with excellent provenance; Marchand de Soif, one of the largest shops in town with over 30 open bottles to taste. You'll notice many advertise the same bottles in the windows but some specialize in back vintages, some in rare bottles and some in international wines as well as those from Bordeaux.

Finish up with a trip – and possibly a glass of wine – at Les Cordeliers, a former monastery that is now a sparkling wine producer.

St-Emilion

Day trip 2 Médoc

Visit:

Pauillac
Lynch-Bages
Haut-Bages Libéral
Pichon Baron
Lagrange, St-Julien
Siran
Dauzac
Angludet

Head north out of Bordeaux on the D2, the Route des Châteaux. This fast, scenic route through the towns and villages of the Médoc is possibly the world's most famous wine road, from Margaux to St-Estèphe, passing by the legendary properties – Margaux, Palmer, the Pichons, the Bartons, Lafite and Mouton and dozens more of near-equal renown.

Margaux is closest geographically to Bordeaux so it's the logical first stop. Another option is to drive straight to Pauillac or St-Estèphe (60km, about 1.5 hours), and make your visits on the way back.

If you are intent on bagging only the grands châteaux (see Châteaux tours and tastings pages 118–137), and you plan enough in advance, you may be able to visit Margaux for a tour, or Mouton Rothschild with its unique wine museum and gallery of artist-commissioned bottle labels plus a tasting. Generally visits must be booked at least two months in advance and will last from one to two and a half hours.

For lunch, stop at Café Lavinal in the charming village of Bages, home to Château Lynch-Bages (page 142) and its impressive new glass-clad winery.

After lunch, either stay in Pauillac and visit Pichon Baron, renowned for its impressive architecture – tasting takes place on the new indoor/outdoor terrace – or head south to Lagrange in St-Julien for a look at its cool new tasting room.

Château Mouton Rothschild

Finish your afternoon at the family-owned, non-classified Angludet for an electric buggy vineyard tour and tasting on the outdoor decking.

For dinner, either head up for an overnight stay at Maison d'Estournel in St-Estèphe (see page 162) or return to Bordeaux and dine at either Le Gabriel (see page 147) or L'Univerre, with its 1,300-strong wine list (see page 156).

Day trip 3 Pessac-Léognan

Visit:
Pape Clément
Smith Haut Lafitte
La Mission Haut-Brion
Les Carmes Haut-Brion
La Louvière
Malartic-Lagravière

While the Médoc is flat and relatively featureless but for the grands châteaux and their expansive vineyards, the Graves region is undulating, wooded, dotted with charmingly normal small towns like Léognan, where you'll find a

butcher, baker, tobacconist, small restaurants and cafés.
It's as typically French as you can get.

Drive south from Bordeaux to Pessac-Léognan. Start
with a tour and tasting at Château La Mission Haut-Brion,
one of Bordeaux's oldest and most prestigious wineries,
known for its rich history and exceptional wines; visit
(or stay at) Château Pape Clément, an historic estate
with landscaped gardens and ancient olive trees. It offers
immersive tours and also has accommodation (see Staying
in a Bordeaux château page 160).

For lunch, head to Malartic-Lagravière (its restaurant
was a Best of Wine Tourism winner in 2024), where you
can have a (luxury) picnic: deckchairs and dishes of grilled
meats, seasonal vegetables and three estate wines. For a
more fancy occasion, dine at the château's private residence,
with a special food and wine paired meal curated by the head
chef. Malartic also offers tours and tasting packages.

In the afternoon, visit Château Smith Haut Lafitte,
renowned for its organic winemaking practices and stunning
estate. Take a guided tour and enjoy a tasting session. The
adjacent Les Sources de Caudalie (also part of the family
business) offers a unique wine spa experience if you wish to
indulge further.

Oak vats at Château Pape Clément, Pessac-Léognan

Finish up at Château Carbonnieux, known for its exceptional whites and reds, for drop-in tastings or a guided tour – by appointment only – which looks at centuries-old winemaking traditions.

Drop into wine shop L'Esprit des Vins in Léognan for a great selection of local bottles.

For dinner head to Château Léognan's Le Manège (see page 162); if you want to stay overnight, you might consider one of the château's (surprisingly affordable and rather splendid) wooden lodges or treehouses; or return to Les Sources de Caudalie for a luxurious retreat amidst the vines.

24 hours in Bordeaux
Where to eat and drink (for more details see The Guide page 116)

Wine bars/casual

Les Halles de Bacalan
Soif
L'Univerre
Le Sobre Chartrons
Bacchus
Buvette

Fine dining

Maison Nouvelle
Table de Montaigne
Zéphirine
Le Gabriel

The city of Bordeaux has a dynamic cultural, food and wine scene. It's an excellent base for day trips, and it's a fine, compact, walkable city, with monuments, museums and markets, and Europe's longest shopping street, the busy Rue Sainte-Catherine.

A good place to start the day is at one of the big markets – Halles de Bacalan (open from 8am except Mondays) to

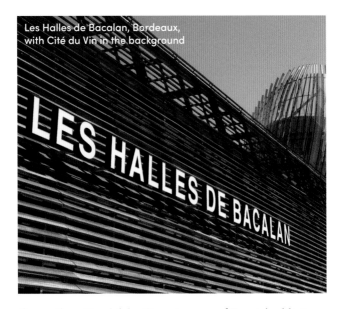

Les Halles de Bacalan, Bordeaux, with Cité du Vin in the background

LES HALLES DE BACALAN

the north or Marché des Capucins, one of France's oldest markets (open 6am to early afternoon) to the south, for their amazing fresh food stalls and endless wine bars – don't miss the oyster bars at Halles de Bacalan.

Near Halles de Bacalan (and a short tram ride from the city centre) is the Cité du Vin. This impressive modernist building (it's supposed to mimic the swirl of wine in a glass) is dedicated to the world of wine, with interactive exhibits, multimedia displays and tastings covering the history of wine, the science of winemaking, cultural practices, and the role of wine in different societies. The Belvédère Bar on the 8th floor has panoramic views of the city; Restaurant Le 7; and Latitude20, a brasserie and bar on the ground floor.

The vibrant Rue Sainte-Catherine is Europe's longest shopping street and a good way to spend a couple of hours before sampling a variety of Bordeaux wines (at all levels) at Le Bar à Vin at the CIVB (see page 157). This is a Bordeaux institution – and as the CIVB represents every Bordeaux appellation it can be an excellent primer on a vast variety of wine produced here. On the ground floor of the triangular 18th-century Maison Gobineau, a couple of steps away from the Grand Théâtre, it's one of the largest wine bars in Bordeaux.

There are dozens of restaurants to choose from in the evening (see page 144) from the traditional and hearty fire-cooked fare of La Tupina to the friendly Brasserie Bordelaise. Be sure to stop at Aux Quatre Coins du Vin for a great wine list and tasting options from the Enomatic machines; other among many options include Symbiose for cocktails, and the relaxed Yarra (run by an Australian-French couple), which has a good selection of international wines.

A week in Bordeaux

A week is perfect to explore Bordeaux. It gives you the opportunity to explore the seaside: **Arcachon Bay** for oysters and dry white wine, and a walk around the lively town, or chic Cap Ferret for a wonderful daily market and an exhilarating tumble in the Atlantic waves. There's a ferry that connects the two if you wanted to visit both, but save at least a day for each. There's also the 100-metre-high **Dune du Pilat** (Europe's highest sand dune), which takes an hour to climb. Take a picnic.

Stay a few nights in Bordeaux city and drive to the Médoc from there and a few nights in St-Emilion, or make daily trips from a Bordeaux base. St-Estèphe to the north, St-Emilion to the south-east and Sauternes to the south-west are each roughly an hour to an hour and a half away.

With seven days, you could easily fill two days exploring the Médoc and its châteaux, one day in **Pessac-Léognan** walking or cycling, two days in **St-Emilion** (at least half a day in the town itself) and its surrounds, one day in Bordeaux city and one day at the beach. You could factor in half a day in **Sauternes** and one visit in the **Entre-Deux-Mers** too, depending on how much driving you want to do and how many tastings you'd like to fit in.

Day 1: Arrival and Explore Bordeaux

Morning:

- **Stay:** Check-in at Maison Labruyère in the heart of Bordeaux city. Owned by the same family as Pomerol's Château Rouget, home-like comfort in a hotel.
- **Activity:** Explore Rue Sainte-Catherine, Europe's longest shopping street and study the wine offering at the renowned wine shop **L'Intendant Grands Vins de Bordeaux**, next to the Intercontinental Hotel.

Afternoon:

- **Lunch:** Oysters and white wine at Les Halles de Bacalan.
- **Activity:** Visit the **Cité du Vin** wine museum.

Evening:

- **Dinner:** Experience Bordeaux's historic Chartrons neighbourhood with dinner at **Cent 33**, an eco-friendly focus with vegetables from its own city garden.

Day 2: The Médoc

Morning:

- **Activity:** Drive to the Médoc on the D2 Route des Châteaux for a **Château Margaux** tour (see Châteaux tours and tastings, page 118) . Explore the vineyards and cellars, and learn about the winemaking process.

Afternoon:

- **Lunch:** Enjoy a meal at **Au Marquis de Terme** in Margaux. Savour dishes that blend local Bordeaux ingredients paired with wines from the estate.
- **Activity:** Continue with a visit to **Château Lynch-Bages**. Explore their new cellar facilities, do a tasting and explore the village of Bages, renovated as a model village by the late Jean-Michel Cazes.

Evening:
- **Dinner: Café Lavinal** at Château Lynch-Bages, brasserie-style dishes and an extensive wine list.
- **Stay: Château Cordeillan-Bages**, a Relais & Châteaux hotel in the vineyards.

Day 3: St-Emilion

Morning:
- **Activity:** St-Emilion is a UNESCO World Heritage Site. Take a guided tour of the medieval town and its many historic monuments.

Afternoon:
- **Lunch: La Terrasse Rouge** at Château La Dominique, with its panoramic views of the vineyards.
- **Activity: Château Angelus** for a wine tasting and tour of the estate; drop into **Le Dôme** next door – built by Norman Foster for the original *garagiste* Jonathan Maltus, it looks like a UFO has landed gently in the vineyards.

Evening:
- **Dinner:** Enjoy a gourmet dinner at **Les Belles Perdrix**, Château Troplong Mondot's renowned restaurant on the highest point in the appellation.
- **Stay:** Check into **Logis de la Cadène**, a Michelin-starred restaurant with rooms, owned by Château Angelus.

Day 4: Pessac-Léognan

Morning:
- **Activity:** Pessac-Léognan for a visit to **Château Smith Haut Lafitte**. Take a tour of the vineyards and the winemaking facilities.

Afternoon:

- **Lunch:** Picnic lunch at **Château Malartic-Lagravière** before or after a tour and tasting at the estate.
- **Activity:** Explore the nearby **Château La Mission Haut-Brion** or **Pape Clément**, two of the oldest and most prestigious wineries in Bordeaux.

Evening:

- **Dinner: La Table du Lavoir** at Les Sources de Caudalie (more casual) or **La Grand'Vigne** (two Michelin stars).
- **Stay:** Stay at Les Sources de Caudalie, part of the Château Smith Haut Lafitte estate.

Day 5: Arcachon Bay and Cap Ferret

Morning:

- **Activity:** Take a boat tour of the bay, including a visit to the **Ile aux Oiseaux** and the famous oyster farms.

Afternoon:

- **Lunch:** Fresh seafood at **Chez Pierre**, a well-known restaurant in Arcachon.
- **Activity:** Spend the afternoon relaxing on the beach or climbing the Grande Dune du Pilat.

Evening:

- **Dinner:** Dine at Michelin-starred **Le Skiff Club** at Hotel Ha(a)ïtza in Pyla-sur-Mer.
- **Stay:** Boutique **Hotel Ville d'Hiver** in Arcachon.

Day 6: Cap Ferret

Morning:

- **Activity:** Drive to Cap Ferret. Explore the village and its lighthouse.

Afternoon:

- **Lunch:** Enjoy lunch at **La Maison du Bassin**, cosy and renowned for its seafood.
- **Activity:** Spend the afternoon at the beach or take a bike ride through the pine forests.

Evening:

- **Dinner:** Have dinner at **Le Pinasse Café**, beautiful views and delicious seafood.
- **Stay:** Stay at the charming **Hôtel des Dunes**.

Day 7: Return to Bordeaux

Morning:

- **Activity:** Explore Bordeaux's markets, such as **Marché des Capucins** and pick up a bargain at the nearby flea market at St-Michel.

Afternoon:

- **Lunch:** Enjoy lunch at **Le Quatrième Mur**, a contemporary brasserie inside the Grand Théâtre by Michelin-starred chef Philippe Etchebest.
- **Activity:** Visit the **Musée d'Aquitaine** to learn more about the history and culture of the region.

Evening:

- **Dinner:** Dine at **Le Gabriel**, a Michelin-starred restaurant located in the heart of Bordeaux within sight of the quay.
- **Stay:** Stay at **Le Grand Hotel**, Bordeaux's smartest hotel, opposite the opera house for a luxurious end to the trip.

On two wheels at Marquis de Terme, Margaux

LISTINGS PREPARED BY

Carolyn Boyd
Nina Caplan
James Lawrence
Tina Meyer
Laura Richards

The Guide

Contents

CLUB OENOLOGIQUE

The Guide is produced in partnership with Club Oenologique, the premium lifestyle publication connecting people to the joys of the world through the lens of wine and spirits

Scan for the latest on Bordeaux, and expert guides to food and drink regions around the world

Châteaux tours and tastings

Bordeaux cast off its buttoned-up image long ago. In the last decade it has embraced the spirit of immersive tourism – from north to south and east to west, there are hundreds of châteaux at every level offering tastings, tours and much more.

Château Smith Haut Lafitte, Pessac-Léognan

Bordeaux, with its exceptional soils, may have mastered the art of turning grapes into fine wine, but it was the Californians who demonstrated the importance of showcasing that viticultural prowess. Indeed, while New World regions flung open their cellar doors in the 20th century, Bordeaux remained somewhat aloof. Behind the elegant palladian façades of the châteaux they gave little thought to the end consumer, preferring to leave the business of marketing to the city's négociants.

'The iconic vineyards of the Médoc, Pessac-Léognan and St-Emilion now challenge tradition with glass-fronted tasting rooms, multilingual tours, Michelin-starred dining rooms and luxurious accommodation'

That was the situation until the early 2000s, when global demand rocketed. Suddenly, the largest fine wine district on Earth was dealing with a new type of wine lover: younger, tech-savvy and insatiably curious about the how and why of viticulture. 'We had to open our doors, share the stories of our wines, and show a different side to Lafite that was not all about men in suits and white-tablecloth restaurants,' CEO Saskia de Rothschild once said.

Thus, the iconic vineyards of the Médoc, Pessac-Léognan and St-Emilion now challenge tradition with glass-fronted tasting rooms, multilingual tours, Michelin-starred dining rooms and luxurious accommodation among the vines. The motor of the fine wine world, hitherto buttoned-up, has embraced the spirit of immersive tourism, blurring the boundaries between visitor and vigneron. Now, visitors can help with the harvest, blend their own *grand vin*, cycle through the vineyards, or simply imbibe. Today in Bordeaux, anything is possible.

Lynch-Bages

Château Phélan Ségur, St-Estèphe

Rue des Écoles, 33180
St-Estèphe, France

It may be a bit of a journey from Bordeaux centre, but a trip to Phélan in St-Estèphe is well worth it. Not only is it a beautiful château in exceptional grounds, but it has breathtaking views over the Gironde. There are interactive tours, with tastings, for budding wine enthusiasts to see what it's like being a vineyard manager or cellar master.

www.phelansegur.com/en

Château Lynch-Bages, Pauillac

33250 Pauillac, France

Restored to its current glory by the indefatigable Jean-Michel Cazes, Lynch-Bages continues to produce benchmark Pauillac: virile, structured and long-lived claret. The château offers a guided tour of its extensive facilities. However, the bespoke options are of far greater interest to experienced oenophiles. These may include a comparative tasting of Lynch-Bages and other significant Pauillacs, a blending masterclass, food and wine pairings, or a picnic in the vines. The family also run Relais & Châteaux hotel Cordeillan-Bages and Café Lavinal, both in the vicinity.

www.lynchbages.com/en

Château Pichon Baron, Pauillac

D2, 33250 Pauillac, France

It takes a stony heart to not be captivated by Pichon Baron's fairytale castle, or indeed the luxurious visitor centre and tasting room – more Napa Valley than Gironde. For over 350 years, Pauillac's leading Second Growth has been producing some of the Médoc's most powerful and structured Cabernet-Merlot blends. Explore the nuances of terroir, weather

Pichon Baron

and climate by booking a vertical tasting of four vintages – currently the 2010, 2016, 2018 and 2019.

www.pichonbaron.com/en

Château Haut-Bages Libéral, Pauillac

18 Balogues, 33250 Pauillac, France

Steered by the incredibly talented Claire Villars-Lurton, Haut-Bages Libéral is the jewel in the Lurton family crown – 30 hectares of prime vineyards situated at the heart of the Médoc. But it's not all work and no play here; visitors are invited to explore the château's vineyards and premises before enjoying a vertical and/or horizontal tasting as a precursor to a gourmet lunch. People rave about the 'Discovering Grand Cru' masterclass where guests compare and contrast the best of Bordeaux with a Sonoma Cabernet from an estate also owned by G&C Lurton Estates.

www.gc-lurton-estates.com/en/château-haut-bages-liberal.html

Haut-Bages Libéral

Château Lagrange, St-Julien

33250 Saint-Julien-Beychevelle, France

Sip Merlot straight from the barrel at Third Growth Château Lagrange, or even ponder the alchemy of wine via an in-depth blending workshop hosted by a member of the cellar team. This historic estate (founded in the 1700s) became a part of the Suntory group in 1983, which goes towards explaining its elevated, immersive wine tourism options. There is also an opportunity to take part in the annual harvest, followed by a picnic in the château's exquisite grounds.

www.château-lagrange.com

Château Léoville Poyferré, St-Julien

38 Rue de Saint-Julien, 33250 Saint-Julien-Beychevelle, France

Owned and run by the Cuvelier family for over 100 years, in the 17th century it was part of the same estate as Léoville Barton and Léoville Las Cases, and its wines are as seductive and voluptuous as any in St-Julien. It offers tailor-made tours, light lunches on the terrace, cycling through the vines with gourmet snacks, a panoramic appellation tasting, pairing wine with chocolate; or an immersion into Poyferré itself with three

mature vintages showing the nuances and subtleties of these great wines. A popular cruise-ship destination with tours in both English and French and a private dining room that can accommodate up to 15 guests for a seated meal.

www.leoville-poyferre.fr

Château Beychevelle, St-Julien

33250 Saint-Julien-Beychevelle, France

Château Beychevelle has been dubbed the 'Versailles of the Médoc' on account of its majestic architecture and beautiful gardens (including a magnificent 200-year-old cedar). It's rather wonderful to stand on the terrace with a glass of wine and look down over the formal garden to the Gironde in the distance. The property has a 300-year-old lineage, the home of aristocrats and patrons of the arts (Molière came here). The guided tours of the vineyard, winery and the château itself give an excellent flavour of Bordeaux at its grandest.

www.beychevelle.com

Château d'Issan, St-Julien

Chem. de la Ménagerie, 33460 Margaux-Cantenac, France

Arguably one of the most beautiful Bordeaux estates,

Beychevelle

the moated d'Issan has a winemaking past going back to the 12th century – its wines were served at the wedding of Henry Plantagenet and Eleanor of Aquitaine in 1152. The original château was demolished in the 1700s to make way for the very fine current building, which retains some of the original medieval features, such as the dramatic gateway, the towers and moat. Tours take you around the château and vineyard. A fascinating glimpse both into Bordeaux's distant past and its present.

www.château-issan.com

d'Issan

Château d'Arsac, Margaux

33460 Arsac, France

Many wineries like to show off their art collections but Château d'Arsac takes it very seriously, with a sculpture garden showcasing works by major French abstract and conceptual artists such as Bernard Pagès, Claude Viallat and Bernar Venet, among many others. Previous owner Philippe Raoux was also deeply into what he called 'oeno-music' – one of the tours includes a sound and light show in the barrel cellars. D'Arsac is interesting for other reasons – Raoux was fascinated by terroir and his 'Winemaker's Collection' bottling takes the same terroir but changes the winemaker each year. A different experience and well worth the visit.

www.château-arsac.com

Château Dauzac, Margaux

Av. Georges Johnston, 33460 Labarde, France

Tours, tastings, picnics, cooking classes, weddings and overnight stays in a gorgeous five-bedroom *chartreuse*. Plus, a shop filled with merchandize adorned with the signature yellow label. Château Dauzac should be your first stop as you leave Bordeaux on the D2. The estate also has an impressively large range of wines including the innovative ungrafted Franc de Pied Cabernet Sauvignon.

www.châteaudauzac.com

Château Giscours, Margaux

10 Rte de Giscours, 33460 Labarde, France

Giscours is one of the easiest of the great châteaux to get to – about half an hour from the centre of Bordeaux. It won the top tourism award from the organization Great Wine Capitals in 2024 and it's not hard to see why. This 300-hectare Margaux estate is a majestic setting for exploring behind the scenes of a Grand Cru Classé. You can eat produce grown and bred on site in the grand dining room of the château; the guest rooms are in the old stables overlooking the vineyards. Visitors can tour the vast park and forest – it's a working farm so no dogs are allowed – and finish with a tasting for €10.

www.giscours.com/fr

Château du Tertre, Margaux

14 Allée du Tertre, 33460 Arsac, France

A 1,000-year-old estate with a 50-metre outdoor pool and adjoining orangerie in the heart of the Médoc. Château du Tertre, which can trace its history back to the 12th century, has four bedrooms for overnighters and offers visits and tastings (it has one of the few Margaux white wines – Château Margaux's Pavillon Blanc being the most famous). A rare glimpse into old-world Bordeaux.

www.châteaudutertre.fr

Château Siran, Margaux

13 Av. du Comté JB Lynch, 33460 Labarde, France

It's possible that Siran flies somewhat under the radar in the famous Margaux region. This beautiful *chartreuse* has been run by the same family since 1859, responsible for producing quintessential Margaux: elegant, understated and perfumed. Not only does it house an extensive collection of *objets d'art* displayed in the new Chai des Collections, Siran is also the only Médoc château to own an anti-atomic bunker – 30,000 bottles are stored in this subterranean labyrinth, where tastings can be carried out. Down in 'Le Bunker', you can even book an escape room experience and attempt to decipher the secrets of this family estate before the clock runs out.

www.châteausiran.com/en/château-siran-margaux

Siran

Angludet

Château Angludet, Margaux
33460 Margaux-Cantenac, France

Château Angludet is a family-run property widely acknowledged for producing classed-growth-quality wines at reasonable prices. Its delicious, structured blends have long been popular in the UK, and you can now enjoy the wines on the property's spectacular terrace, complete with views of the surrounding countryside. Most visitors rely on Bernadette, the château's electric buggy, to whizz them around the estate before sampling a trio of exceptional vintages.

www.sichel.fr/en/vineyards-maison-sichel/château-angludet.html

Château Ferrière, Margaux
33 bis Rue de la Tremoille, 33460 Margaux-Cantenac, France

Ferrière has long been one of Margaux's most powerful and dense red wines. This beautiful property takes its

Ferrière

name from Gabriel Ferrière, a parliamentarian and merchant who owned the estate in the 1700s. Today it is run (like Haut-Bages Libéral) with flair and energy by Claire Villars-Lurton. Visitors are encouraged to stroll through its vines and learn the secrets of biodynamic viticulture, before raising a glass to the magic of the Médoc and its gravel terroir.

www.gc-lurton-estates.com/en/château-Ferrière.html

Château du Taillan, Haut-Medoc

56 Av. de la Croix, 33320 Le Taillan-Médoc, France

If there's such a thing as a feminist Bordeaux château, du Taillan is it. Owned by five sisters, members of the Cruse family, one of Bordeaux's most

Where winemakers dine

TentaziOni is a very beautiful Italian gourmet restaurant – they won a Michelin star in 2020 and produce amazing Italian gourmet tasting menus which change weekly. All their dishes are prepared on-site and use ultra-fresh market produce. They have the best champagne and Italian Bordeaux wine list and a very fine selection of Bordeaux wines. **Ressources** is another excellent choice: an innovative French Michelin-starred restaurant with a very good French wine list. The chef is technically brilliant, producing a selection of daring and delicious small plates. **Point Rouge**, meanwhile, is one of Europe's largest and most elite cocktail bars. The bar offers a diverse selection of expertly crafted cocktails, often featuring unique ingredients and novel flavour combinations. It should also be noted that they have a fine European wine list, including wines from Domaine Clarence Dillon.

Jean-Philippe Delmas, Domaine Clarence Dillon (Châteaux Haut-Brion, La Mission Haut-Brion and Quintus)

prominent wine dynasties, it is run by the fourth-generation Armelle Cruse. 'This is a story of women' the website says, stressing the 'feminine aura' of the beautiful 18th-century property where the sisters grew up. 'Even the mechanical harvester' is operated by a woman, Jane Anson notes in *Inside Bordeaux*. Guided tours are comprehensive and you can picnic in the grounds; Château du Taillan hosts events and exhibitions, making it a vibrant cultural hub, and participates in the annual *Portes Ouvertes* 'open doors' weekend.

www.châteaudutaillan.com

Château Pape Clément, Pessac-Léognan

216 Av. Dr Nancel Penard, 33600 Pessac, France

The wines of Pessac-Léognan have a far longer history than those of the Médoc: Pape Clément was established in the 1300s and bequeathed to the archbishop Bertrand de Goth, subsequently Pope Clement V of Avignon. Today, it is renowned for its seductive red blend and voluptuous, oak-aged Bordeaux Blanc, overseen by the wine tycoon Bernard Magrez. Under his direction, the property has become a beacon of luxury tourism, offering a broad variety of experiences – including a

vertical tasting of five vintages – and accommodation in the ornate castle.

www.château-pape-clement.fr/en

Château Smith Haut Lafitte, Pessac-Léognan

33650 Martillac, France

For over two decades, owners Daniel and Florence Cathiard have run a luxurious hotel, two restaurants and a thermal spa at this Grand Cru Classé estate to international acclaim. To immerse yourself, literally, you can try a red-wine bath or Cabernet body scrub, said to promote anti-ageing, at Les Sources de Caudalie. But for those more interested in drinking the stuff, the estate also offers a number of masterclasses and workshops, including the popular 'Caviar from sea and soil' – an extensive tour that's finished with the house's *grand vin* paired with Sturia caviar.

www.smith-haut-lafitte.com/en

Château La Mission Haut-Brion, Pessac-Léognan

67 Rue de Peybouquey, 33400 Talence, France

La Mission Haut-Brion has been producing red wine since the late Middle Ages. Today, it is one of the few Grand Cru

La Mission Haut-Brion

Classé properties to offer an extensive tour free of charge: you'll visit the magnificent Salle des Vignes, entirely decorated by owner Prince Robert of Luxembourg, before strolling through its formal gardens. Thereafter, visit the 1,000 sq m cellar before enjoying a glass of La Mission Haut-Brion in the beautiful tasting room decorated with a collection of engravings by Albrecht Dürer. If your own collecting is limited to wine, the estate boutique sells an extensive back catalogue of venerable vintages.

There is no charge for the tour. Reservations can be made via this link.

www.mission-haut-brion.com/en

Château Malartic-Lagravière, Pessac-Léognan

43 Av. de Mont de Marsan, 33850 Léognan, France

Owned and run by the Bonnie family since 1997, this grand (but very friendly) Graves estate is at the forefront of Bordeaux hospitality. Not only do they make very good – and good value – red and white wines, the expertly curated tourism programme is internationally acclaimed. There are 10 different options including classic and private visits as well as cheese and wine matching, picnics on the lawn, a walking tour around the estate and a gourmet food and wine experience during the chef's workshop. There really is something for everyone.

www.malartic-lagraviere.com

Malartic-Lagravière

Château Haut-Bailly, Pessac-Léognan

48 Rue de la Liberté, 33850 Léognan, France

One of the most beautiful estates in Bordeaux, American-owned Haut-Bailly opened its stunning new ultra-sustainable, mostly underground winery in 2020. Various visits are on offer including private tours or gourmet experiences with a tasting. The 19th-century château has five bedrooms, and there's the nearby 18th-century Chartreuse Haut-Bailly (formerly known as Le Pape), recently renovated. Luxury in the Graves.

www.haut-bailly.com

Château Les Carmes Haut-Brion, Pessac-Léognan

20 Rue des Carmes, 33000 Bordeaux, France

A few tram stops from Bordeaux's city centre lies Les Carmes Haut-Brion. It has been part of the Haut-Brion estate for 400 years; now with whizz-kid winemaker Guillaume Pouthier (voted best winemaker in France by *Le Figaro*) and Philippe Starck-designed winery (it famously resembles an upside-down ship), it's one of the most celebrated and coolest properties on the Left Bank.

www.les-carmes-haut-brion. com/fr

Château La Louvière, Pessac-Léognan

149 Av. de Cadaujac, 33850 Léognan, France

The Lurton family is one of Bordeaux's most prominent wine dynasties, owning more than 20 properties including several Grand Cru Classés. The genial Jacques Lurton (cousin of Pierre, who runs Château d'Yquem and Cheval Blanc) is in charge of six properties in four different appellations. One of these is the warm and welcoming Château La Louvière in Pessac-Léognan. You can tour the grounds and cellars, do an 'epicurean' tasting or blend your own wine after sampling from barrel. This comes highly recommended.

www.andrelurton.com/en/ château/château-la-louviere

Château de Rouillac, Pessac-Léognan

12 Chem. du 20 Août 1949, 33610 Canéjan, France

The architectural splendour of Château de Rouillac is the work of Baron Haussman, the French civic planner who oversaw the transformation of Paris in the 19th century. He created the building's stunning façade, courtyard, landscaped spaces, stables and orangerie. The estate is committed to sustainable agriculture, integrating eco-friendly practices in its vineyards and production processes – the château also has a prestigious horse breeding and training facility; a visit to the stables is included in the tour. This combination of fine wine, history and equestrianism makes for an interesting and unusual visit.

www.châteauderouillac.com

Château Sigalas Rabaud, Sauternes

1 Rabaud-Sigalas, 33310 Bommes, France

Sauternes châteaux are super-keen on hospitality and the award-winning, sixth-generation-run Sigalas Rabaud is one of the best. The fine, honey-coloured low-lying house is exceptionally pretty, and it has a variety of visits on offer with a series of different tastings. There's also the option to privatize a trip, include a gourmet food offering for lunch or dinner, and bed and breakfast stay in one of five guest rooms in the family's 17th-century *chartreuse*. The (perhaps unfortunately named) Marie Antoinette room has views of Château d'Yquem.

www.château-sigalas-rabaud.com

Château Suduiraut, Sauternes

Suduiraut, 33210 Preignac, France

It is hard to imagine a more beautiful château than the imposing castle at Suduiraut. Built in the 17th century, the property is surrounded by expansive gardens designed

Suduiraut

Soutard

by King Louis XIV's landscape architect, André Le Nôtre. Yet the hospitality is thoroughly warm and unpretentious at this Premier Cru Sauternes estate. Guided tours can end with either a standard tasting or, even better, a cheese-and-wine pairing in the modern visitor room. Suduiraut also produces an increasing volume of dry white wines, including a delectable 100% Sémillon Blanc.

www.suduiraut.com

Château Guiraud, Sauternes

1 Château Guiraud, 33210 Sauternes, France

In the centre of this Sauternes property stands the imposing château with its panelled salons. It is surrounded by extensive gardens that support a huge variety of flora and fauna;

biodiversity is of supreme importance to this First Growth estate, the first among the top tier to be certified organic back in 2011. Several imaginative tours are available, including a cycle tour through the vines before a tutored tasting of three distinct vintages of Guiraud. There is also an excellent on-site restaurant and wine bar, La Chapelle, which serves a daily lunch menu for under €30 per person.

www.châteauguiraud.com/en

Château Soutard, St-Emilion

33330 St-Emilion, France

This imposing and ancient château stands on top of the St-Emilion plateau – Soutard dates back to 1513, although the fine buildings we see today are from the 18th century.

The whole property has been extensively renovated (it won the Best of Bordeaux Wine Tourism prize a few years ago). A variety of visits is on offer, from bicycle tours of the vineyards and surrounding countryside to cellar tastings and more in-depth hour-long masterclasses on winemaking, the importance of barrels and so on. Well worth it, especially as you can have a glass of wine on the terrace after your visit.

www.château-soutard.com/visites

Le Dôme, St-Emilion

1 Les Verdiannes Lieu dit, 33330 St-Emilion, France

One of the most striking examples of modern architecture in Bordeaux, Le Dôme is a circular winery conceived by architect-to-the-wine-stars Norman Foster for St-Emilion renegade Jonathan Maltus. The building is right next door to the vineyards of Angelus (Le Dôme was one of the original *garagiste* wines). It looks rather like a spaceship which has dropped down among the vines; a wraparound walkway takes you up to a marvellous tasting room with 360-degree views. Its most affordable tour visits the winery, while the next tier up explores the story of the region's *garagiste* movement, of which Maltus was

at the centre. Alternatively, the winery's 'A to Z' masterclass offers a workshop that gets down to the nitty-gritty of wine enjoyment with comparative tastings of freshly opened bottle versus decanted wines, and advice on the selection of glassware, storage and service.

www.ledome-saintemilion.com

Château de Ferrand, St-Emilion

Allée de Saint-Poly, Saint-Hippolyte, 33330 St-Emilion, France

This 18th-century château is owned by the heirs of Baron Bich, of Bic ballpoint fame; it was beautifully renovated in 2019, and has since won prizes for its oenotourism offering. This includes a

multitude of viticultural and gastronomic experiences, from a tasting and lunch in the orangerie to a macaron-making workshop or sommelier-led masterclass in food-and-wine pairing. A major draw is the wealth of artwork (many by world-famous artists), all using the Bic pen; there are dozens of sculptures, including a giant chewed pen-top at the entrance. Guest suites and reception rooms are luxurious old-world château style. A simply delightful getaway.

www.châteaudeferrand.com/en

Château La Dominique, St-Emilion

1 La Dominique, 33330 St-Emilion, France

The voluptuous, Merlot-dominant wines of Château La Dominique are as famous in Bordeaux as the property's handsome restaurant La Terrasse Rouge. The estate is highly popular with those touring St-Emilion, particularly as it serves mature vintages alongside chocolate made by local artisan Chocolaterie Maëlig. Afterwards, take an apéritif at the restaurant and peruse a menu that champions the best of the south west.

www.château-ladominique. com/en/accueil

Château Bellefont-Belcier, St-Emilion

33330 Saint-Laurent-des-Combes, France

Owned by Hong Kong tycoon Peter Kwok (who is much liked by his senior executives), this 18th-century mansion in landscaped gardens is a good way to enjoy the art of living à la Bordelaise. Just outside St-Emilion village, Bellefont-Belcier is a nicely appointed property with tennis court and swimming pool. Private and customized tours and tasting experiences are also available. You can also stay at its sister establishment Tour Saint Christophe, where you get a private terrace and fine vineyard views.

www.vignoblesk.com/en/our-properties/château-bellefont-belcier.aspx

Château Fleur Cardinale, St-Emilion

48 Chemin de Champy, 33330 Saint-Étienne-de-Lisse, France

This Grand Cru Classé estate five minutes' drive from the centre of St-Emilion offers a sensorial experience in viticulture and oenology, with guided tours through the vineyard, vat house and barrel cellar. Biodiversity and sustainability are integral to the winemaking philosophy at Fleur Cardinale, which began organic conversion in 2021. This is a really delightful tasting experience (there are stunning views of the vineyards from a landscaped terrace) and an educational journey into responsible wine production.

www.fleurcardinale.com/en

Château Georges 7, Fronsac

1 Le Bergey, 33141 Saillans, France

With only three hectares of vines, Château Georges 7 in Fronsac is the epitome of a boutique winery. Run by Briton Sally Evans, you can visit its modern cellar facilities and eat on its outdoor terrace (perfect for summer sunset apéros). This is an immersive look at the winemaking process and a delightful change from the majesty of the *grands châteaux*.

www.châteaugeorge7.com

Château de Sales, Pomerol

11 Chem. de Sales, 33500 Libourne, France

A really lovely old Pomerol property, de Sales has been in the hands of the Lambert family for five centuries and is officially listed as an historic monument. Under new management since 2017, its wines have been steadily improving. Visits take you

through the château's long and honourable history – it's a big estate, and except for a few hectares lost in the Revolution, its boundaries are the same as they were in 1578.

www.château-de-sales.com

Château Clinet, Pomerol

16 Chemin de Feytit, 33500 Pomerol, France

The much-respected family estate of the friendly and down-to-earth Ronan Laborde, head of the Union des Grands Crus de Bordeaux. Clinet is a fine, almost-rustic red-shuttered manor house in the Pomerol style. Visitors are taken through the story of the estate since the 17th century with vineyard visits, a tour of the modern cellars and guided tastings.

www.châteauclinet.com

Château Bonalgue and Château Clos du Clocher, Pomerol

24 Rue de Bonalgue, 33500 Libourne, France
57 Rue de Catusseau, 33500 Pomerol, France

If you're in Pomerol you shouldn't miss a tasting at Clos du Clocher, or an overnight stay at the charming Bonalgue. Both are owned by Jean-Baptiste Bourotte, whose family celebrated 100 years of Pomerol winemaking in 2024. Friendly and open, the whole team is knowledgeable and full of passion for their wines (there are parcels of Cabernet Franc over 60 years old – which is ancient for Bordeaux).

www.domainesbourotteaudy.fr

Château L'Evangile, Pomerol

2 Chem. de Maillet, 33500 Pomerol, France

Rothschild-owned and so Lafite's sister estate, Château L'Evangile has some of the most sought-after wines in the Pomerol appellation. The tours (only by appointment) are a deep dive into the winemaking process from vineyard to fermentation to ageing. The château is celebrated for its terroir and for its commitment to organic and biodynamic farming. One of Pomerol's most serious and renowned estates (Jane Anson calls it 'an insider's Pomerol'), this is one for enthusiasts.

www.lafite.com/domaines/château-levangile

Château La Fleur de Boüard, Lalande-de-Pomerol

12 Rte de Bertineau, 33500 Néac, France

Purchased by Hubert de Boüard in 1998, Château La

Fleur de Boüard is leading the way in immersive wine tourism in Bordeaux. In the barrel cellar, experience the 'Chai de Lumière', where an audiovisual presentation with historical and modern imagery of the estate, special effects and strobe lighting paints a powerful picture of the story of wine. Visitors can also choose to make their own blend in a workshop with the cellar master. A well-stocked boutique, chic tasting room, sumptuous accommodation and wine bar completes the line-up.

www.lafleurdebouard.com/en/accueil

La Fleur de Boüard

The best châteaux restaurants

They have the greatest cellars in the world and access to some of the finest ingredients (often in their own kitchen gardens). Bordeaux estates are welcoming visitors like never before – and here we list half a dozen châteaux that should be on the list of every wine lover.

Château Petit Faurie de Soutard

Where power and money are found, there is usually good eating – and Bordeaux's hegemony came from wine, itself an agricultural product and one that demands fine food. In his great 1958 book *The Food of France*, Waverley Root describes Sauce Bordelaise (wine, butter, marrow, thyme and nutmeg) but then lists several entirely different dishes that are also described as *à la bordelaise* – an indication of how spoilt for choice the region's inhabitants have always been, with their vast array of wonderful products. And the recent crop of fine-dining restaurants in wine châteaux – who are waking up to the possibilities of oenotourism – confirms that the tradition of using beautiful ingredients to make dishes that glorify some of the world's greatest wines is thriving. There is now great eating in châteaux from Sauternes to the northern reaches of the Médoc, and perhaps especially in St-Emilion, where a closer look at even the oldest eating establishment, Le Logis de la Cadène (founded 1848) reveals a château connection: this Michelin-starred restaurant with rooms is owned by Stéphanie de Boüard-Rivoal, president of one of Bordeaux's finest estates, Château Angelus.

The restaurants listed here benefit from the kinds of cellars that can be mustered by people who have been making fabulous wines for generations – sometimes for centuries. Some are attached to hotels, which is especially useful for avoiding any need to drink First Growths and drive; all are surrounded by vineyards, and run by chefs determined to offer visitors the best possible gastronomic experience of the region. For centuries, the Bordelais viewed a knock on the château door as an intrusion, acceptable only if the intruder wished to taste swiftly, buy copiously and depart precipitately. That is no longer how wine lovers behave and the great châteaux have adjusted their actions to suit their clientele, just as they have been doing for hundreds of years – a habit that has probably been as instrumental in their success as the marvels of their terroir.

Where winemakers dine

One of my favourite destinations is **Inima**: it serves floral and vegetable-led cuisine, and is owned by a self-made female chef, Oxana Crétu, who worked very hard to get her first Michelin star. **Shasha sur le Toit**, a rooftop restaurant that opens from May to October, is another excellent choice: delicious Mediterranean cuisine, unsurpassed views of the Garonne, and a good selection of cocktails. Lastly, **El Nacional** is a very popular Argentinian restaurant at the heart of the Chartrons district – it is almost an institution for meat lovers, and the wine list is excellent too.

**Gwendeline Lucas,
Château La Dominique**

Les Sources de Caudalie

La Grand'Vigne at Les Sources de Caudalie, Château Smith Haut Lafitte, Martillac

Former ski champions Daniel and Florence Cathiard bought this wine estate in the 1990s, but it was their daughters, Alice and Mathilde, who made the property as famous for hospitality as for wine, with luxury hotel Les Sources de Caudalie and a line of grape-based health products that is now global. But it's not all skin food: the hotel has the two-Michelin-starred La Grand'Vigne, where Nicolas Masse takes full and inventive advantage of the bounty of Aquitaine, including the wines, which he uses as infusion and ingredient as well as accompaniment. There is also more casual food at La Table du Lavoir, constructed (from 18th-century timber from Lafite Rothschild's cellars) around a *lavoir* – the stone communal washing trough once used by women to do their laundry.

www.sources-caudalie.com/en

Le Cercle Guiraud, Sauternes

Château Guiraud was classified as a Sauternes Premier Grand Cru in the famous 1855 hierarchy of Bordeaux vineyards and was the first of those estates to open a restaurant, in the property's former Protestant chapel. Which makes sense: Sauternes is a wonderful food-matching wine that suffers from the mistaken assumption that sweet wine belongs with dessert. The proprietor also has a restaurant in the village of Sauternes, so close (less than a mile away) that it too offers views of the vines. Here, chef Yoann Amado reinterprets French classics as well as serving unclassical sharing plates of charcuterie or taramasalata. Amado trained under triple-Michelin-starred Eric Fréchon, which may explain the chicken with vin jaune and morels on his menu that appears to be a homage to Fréchon's legendary chicken cooked in a bladder, which is a dish that also includes those ingredients. Products are local (sometimes, from the Guiraud kitchen garden) and in addition to pastries made by Juliette Bonnard, there is a wine list overseen by Denis Verneau, who has won the prestigious accolade *Meilleur Ouvrier de France*.

www.châteauguiraud.com/en/#restaurant

Au Marquis de Terme, Château Marquis de Terme, Margaux

This restaurant with modern décor was the first opened by a Margaux château and has everything that a place with that kind of pedigree should. There's a terrace surrounded by the Médoc vineyards; an open kitchen, so that guests can watch chef Grégory Coutanceau work on the dishes that he views as a meeting place between the waters around La Rochelle (where he has several other restaurants) and the Bordeaux landscape; and a wine list showcasing this world-famous terroir. There are frequent Grand Cru dinners, too: a six-course set menu and an opportunity to explore the wines of a specific château, each carefully matched to a dish.

www.au-marquis-de-terme.com

Au Marquis de Terme

La Dominique

Terrasse Rouge, Château La Dominique, St-Emilion

The walls of windows slide back, on warm days, to give direct access to the outdoor area and bring visitors into direct communion with the vines. Which makes this terrace above the cellars an extension of La Dominique's vineyards, encompassing 29 hectares on the Right Bank within hailing distance of legendary wine châteaux La Conseillante and Cheval Blanc. The wine list ranges across France and so intent are the proprietors, and chef François Duchet, on showcasing local ingredients that their producers are actually named in several of the dishes.

www.laterrasserouge.com

Café Lavinal, Château Lynch-Bages, Bages

The Cazes family bought Château Lynch-Bages, overlooking the Gironde estuary, in 1939, and it was the foundation of a wine empire that, under Jean-Michel, expanded to include another six estates reaching as far as Portugal's Douro. Jean-Michel, who died in 2023 at the age of 88, also renovated the village of Bages and opened this charming 1930s-style brasserie, a few steps from Lynch-Bages in one direction and the family's hotel, Château Cordeillan-Bages, in the other. It's very pleasant to sit looking out on the cobbled village square, eating foie gras terrine, scallops or saddle of lamb with a selection from the 1,800-strong wine list, while watching the world pass by. Gabriel Gette's treatment of these classics is more sophisticated than your average village brasserie – but then, Bages is not your average village.

www.jmcazes.com/en/cafe-lavinal

Le Jardin, Château Petit Faurie de Soutard, St-Emilion

Just beyond the beautiful city of St-Emilion sits this estate, a sister property to Château Soutard (see page 133). Le Jardin is a restaurant with an elegant interior and outside tables that look onto the garden (including a kitchen garden) as well as the vineyards. Chef Stéphane Casset's dishes are simple but well executed, with judicious additions from elsewhere such

Petit Faurie de Soutard

as shiitake mushrooms and coconut milk. Wine and food pairing is a game they enjoy here, and with more than 500 wine labels, there is plenty to play with.

www.le-jardin-saint-emilion.fr

Château Fage La Maison des Vignes, Arveyres

Not every château wants to offer guests the aristocratic treatment; at Château Fage, the aim is to make arrivals feel like family. Usefully situated halfway between Bordeaux and St-Emilion, this 19th-century property now has a 26-room hotel, a slender heated pool (open summer only) and a bistro restaurant overseen by Clément Costes, formerly of Le Skiff Club (a restaurant beside Arcachon Bay that currently holds two Michelin stars). In addition to Costes' excellent food – aged beef, fish of the day in wild garlic sauce, candied beetroot – there are interesting tasting options, including a comparison of vineyards fed by the Garonne and Dordogne rivers and one that offers a trio of Merlots from different terroirs. Plus, there are wine- and food-pairing experiences, cooking classes and an option to follow Costes into the kitchen, don chef's whites and actually get involved with meal prep.

www.châteaufage.com/en

Where to dine out in Bordeaux

In the last 25 years, Bordeaux has been transformed into a stunning city; its once-blackened UNESCO-listed architecture has been polished and now the pale-gold limestone walls glow in the Aquitaine sun. Meanwhile, the old industrial docks have been redeveloped into dynamic and attractive waterfronts, such as the Bassins à Flots district, which is also home to the striking, ultra-modern wine museum the Cité du Vin.

Inima

The pace of change for the city's dining scene has been even quicker. In the last five to ten years the traditional, meat-focused restaurants that once lured in those from the wine trade have been replaced by a range of restaurants of every nationality catering to every taste from vegan to old-school carnivore. It's a huge and varied dining scene. Small and intimate fine-dining establishments are led by dynamic young chefs, many of whom have worked abroad and have come to this vibrant part of France to pair new ideas and global styles with the bounty of produce available in the region.

Local expert Anne Lataillade, who writes the blog *Papilles et Pupilles* (*www.papillesetpupilles.fr*), suggests that these restaurants are offering a new 'bistronomic' style of dining; they have rapidly grown in number. 'We have many restaurants where the value for money is good, even excellent. I really like, for example, Zéphirine for the quality of cooking, and for the warm welcome and friendly atmosphere,' she says. She has also witnessed a new wave of global cuisine arriving in the city. 'Korean, Japanese, Mexican, Thai, Levantine cuisine. You can find everything in Bordeaux.'

Alongside these trends, there are still traditional haute cuisine restaurants featuring the food world's biggest names, and who often have the backing of luxury hotel groups. 'In recent years, the city has become attractive to top chefs, those who open restaurants in major global cities. I am thinking, for example, of Pierre Gagnaire [La Grande Maison de Bernard Magrez], Gordon Ramsay [Le Pressoir d'Argent at the Intercontinental] and Masaharu Morimoto [Morimoto at Mondrian Bordeaux Les Carmes],' says Lataillade. 'The Gironde is still waiting for a three-star restaurant,' she however concedes. Meanwhile, other hotel restaurants are investing in showcasing the next generation of culinary talent, such as the five-star Palais Gallien whose restaurant La Table de Montaigne now has British chef Oli Williamson at the helm.

La Table de Montaigne
144 Rue Abbé de l'Épée

It's unusual to see a British chef of Oli Williamson's calibre working in France; the recipient of the prestigious Roux Scholarship has an enviable CV that includes a stint as head chef at The Fat Duck in Bray and as part of the team at Zén in Singapore. Having taken the helm at La Table de Montaigne at five-star hotel Le Palais Gallien in January 2024, he has a chance to shine with his own repertoire, a culmination of many influences gathered through his career. Two example dishes are: pigeon with sand carrots and spices, umeboshi, Chinese master stock, stuffed bao and pigeon sausage; and brill stuffed with scallops, blood orange ponzu, kimchi and white asparagus. All is served by attentive staff in a tranquil and intimate dining room.

www.hotel-palais-gallien-bordeaux.com/restaurant

Zéphirine
62 Rue Abbé de l'Epée

Tucked away on the quiet Rue Abbé de l'Epée, the owners of Zéphirine – chef Romain Corbière, his sister Marie-Zéphirine and her husband Bertrand Arnauld – classify their restaurant as an *'auberge urbaine'* thanks to its laidback setting with a wooden-floored dining room and a discreet rear terrace. Despite the relaxed setting, Zéphirine offers a sophisticated cuisine based on excellent produce and built on chef Corbière's experience working with Alain Ducasse and Joël Robuchon. In a city traditionally known for its meaty menus, the restaurant is a great champion of vegetables, and there is even an *épicerie fine* and *patisserie* on-site to add to the venue's allure.

www.zephirine.fr

La Table de Montaigne

Le Gabriel

10 Place de la Bourse

There are few chefs whose cuisine deserves the ultimate Bordeaux *bonne adresse* of the resplendent Place de la Bourse, but Bertrand Noeureuil has earned his place, working as *chef de cuisine* for Arnaud Donckele for 10 years. Le Gabriel comprises two restaurants with more casual destination Le 1544 on an upper floor. But Michelin-starred L'Observatoire is the jewel in the crown with its inventive menus focused on seafood and superlative views of the broad Garonne River as it glides by.

www.le-gabriel-bordeaux.fr

Maison Nouvelle

11 Rue Rode

Although long-established as a name to know within the country's culinary rankings, Philippe Etchebest's fame has reached new levels thanks to his punchy opinions on TV shows such as France's *Top Chef*. And of course, he's long held a position of esteem within this city thanks to his Le Quatrième Mur restaurant within the Opéra National de Bordeaux. In late 2021, he added to his portfolio with Maison Nouvelle, a showcase for the myriad flavours of southwest France that has already earned one Michelin

Zéphirine

star. It is set on the lively Place du Marché des Chartrons, a trendy district once home to the city's many wine merchants.

www.maison-nouvelle.fr

Cent 33

133 Rue du Jardin Publique

This cosy bistro in the Chartrons district has a strong eco-friendly drive and uses seasonal, local or organic ingredients, much of which is taken from the restaurant's nearby potager garden. At the helm is chef Fabien Beaufour (and his wife Emilie) who has worked in some of the world's best restaurants including The French Laundry and Eleven Madison Park in the US. Springtime dishes include grilled miso black cod with morel mushrooms and vin jaune, or saddle of lamb with Agen prunes, beans and black garlic.

www.cent33.com

Where winemakers dine

In Bordeaux, when choosing a restaurant, you have to think about the wines you're going to share to make the moment perfect. That's why my heart goes out to restaurants that offer savoury, authentic cuisine accompanied by an excellent wine list. Chefs like Vivien Durand at **Le Prince Noir** or Tanguy Laviale with **Ressources** and **Vivants** have this knowledge and this great attention to the wine that accompanies their cuisine. **Le Comptoir Cuisine** and **Le 1925** also have very fine wine lists with a bit of depth for those who want to drink Bordeaux in Bordeaux.

One hour's drive from the city centre, and with breathtaking views, **La Co(o)rniche** is one of the most beautiful places in the world.

**Véronique Sanders,
Château Haut-Bailly**

Inima
48 Rue du Palais Gallien

In 2023, Moldovan-born chef Oxana Cretu re-launched her previous restaurant Cromagnon as Inima (which translates as 'with all my heart' from Moldovan), with a more polished, refined menu of delicate dishes with Japanese influences – and with the clear ambition of gaining a Michelin star. Dishes include scallops and vanilla-infused confit persimmon in a citronella broth; and white chocolate tart with arbutus berries. All served in a refined and contemporary dining room.

www.inimarestaurant.com

Soléna
5 Rue Chauffour

This welcoming Michelin-starred restaurant is a short stroll or tram ride from the city centre but worth the detour for chef Victor Ostronzec's menu of creative dishes and tasting menus with matching wine flights. The cuisine is strictly governed by seasonality – with a particular lean towards seafood and fish – and Ostronzec is consistently reinventing his repertoire according to the top produce he sources locally. Expect excellent, attentive service for its 22 covers inside a stylish dining room featuring Scandinavian design references.

www.solena-restaurant.com

Ro'cha
165 Av. d'Eysines

Franco-Portuguese chef Jean-Luc Rocha, a recipient of the prestigious *Meilleur Ouvrier de France*, returns from a period in the kitchens of Paris to the region in which he first made his name (when he took over from Thierry Marx at Pauillac's Château Cordeillan-Bages back in 2010). This is the first restaurant of his own, one where the glitz is pared-back, the atmosphere relaxed, and menus determined by the seasons and the region's market produce. A short ride on the tram towards the Parc Bordelais is rewarded by excellent cuisine for a fraction of the price found at his previous establishments.

www.rocha-restaurant.fr

Mazal
4 Rue du Puits Descujols

For a change from traditional fine dining, seek out Mazal near the Place de la Bourse. It has a great atmosphere – a mirror ball on the ceiling the marker for this – and a menu that blends the best of France and the Levant. Take a seat at the counter and watch the dynamic chefs create dishes that range from the traditional hummus and labneh, to others that fuse Middle Eastern spices with traditional French ingredients, such as spiced, slow-roasted belly pork with caramelized onion and a touch of horseradish.

www.lemazal.fr

Inima

Avant Comptoir du Palais

2 Place du Palais

Bordeaux's outpost of Avant Comptoir du Palais, a 'bistronomic' trailblazer in Paris led by chef Yves Camdeborde, sees his nephew Julien Camdeborde at the helm and serving an array of tapas-style dishes in a relaxed setting. With a repertoire of some 60 dishes, such as tuna tartare with raspberries, or seaweed-salted potatoes, it'll take you on a journey through some of France's best ingredients. The wine choice celebrates the local with a prominent selection from the southwest of France, but there are a couple of vintages on offer from each French region.

camdeborde.com/les-restaurants/avant-comptoir-du-palais

Au Bistrot

61 Place des Capucins, 51 Rue du Hamel

In the heart of downtown Bordeaux near Capucins market, Au Bistrot is warm and welcoming. Its menu is small but well thought out, with a range of classic fish and meat dishes using locally sourced ingredients. The rustic décor and friendly atmosphere – as well as the robust wine list – make it a popular spot for both locals and tourists. Highlights include duck confit, veal kidney and braised beef shoulder. Take a seat at the bar to watch the chefs in action.

www.aubistrot.fr

La Tupina

6 Rue Prte de la Monnaie

La Tupina, founded by Jean-Pierre Xiradakis in 1968, is a Bordeaux institution renowned for its traditional southwestern French cuisine. In a small street in the old part of Bordeaux, a little way from the city centre in the St-Michel district, with its open fireplaces for cooking, small dining rooms and white tablecloths, it's rustic and inviting. The menu by Franck Audu features simple and hearty dishes such as cassoulet, roasted meat and fish (there's even a vegetarian dish). Paired with an extensive wine list (although they also do corkage), La Tupina offers an authentic taste of Bordeaux's regional culinary heritage. Arrive hungry.

www.latupina.com

Le Chapon Fin
5 Rue Montesquieu

Some might say you haven't been to Bordeaux unless you've eaten at Le Chapon Fin. 'Mythical' is often used to describe this epicurean indulgence which once counted wealthy wine merchants, crowned heads of Europe and great names such as Sarah Bernhardt and Toulouse-Lautrec as clients. Founded in 1825, it was one of the first 33 restaurants crowned by Michelin in 1933. Today owned by Sylvie Cazes of St-Emilion Grand Cru Classé estate Château Chauvin, it is known almost as much for its unusual décor as for its food – the dining room is dominated by great outcrops of constructed rock. Chef Younesse Bouakkaoui blends traditional and modern French cuisine, and there's an impressive (Bordeaux) wine list. A true Bordeaux experience.

www.chapon-fin.com

L'Entrecôte
4 Cours du 30 Juillet

In the middle of town, the no-reservation restaurant L'Entrecôte is famous for its simple and delicious formula: steak frites. The twice-daily queues (full of locals) that disappear around the corner are testament to the popularity of this (another!) Bordeaux institution. Inside, eager diners tuck into thinly sliced steak cooked to preference, unlimited crispy fries and the renowned secret sauce, served with a simple salad and robust and tasty house wine. If you still have room you can finish your meal with a selection of classic French desserts.

www.entrecote.fr

Maison Nouvelle

British chef Oli Williamson at La Table de Montaigne

10 top wine bars and bistros in Bordeaux

Bordeaux is packed with excellent wine bars – and they don't necessarily focus on the wines of the region. In fact, in recent years, wine lists have tended to look towards other parts of France and even the rest of the world for inspiration.

The CIVB wine bar, Bordeaux

The high price of some of the most prestigious Bordeaux wine labels has something to do with this. Few bars can afford to offer First and Second Growths to their guests. Such *cuvées* are often allocated in limited quantities and to a different kind of establishment, typically reserved for high-end restaurants or to be tasted directly at the estate (and by prior reservation). Of course, there are some exceptions, with just a few gems listed here that offer wines by the glass or bottle from the top Bordeaux châteaux.

'Many top bars offer a vast selection of wine by the glass – sometimes listing up to 40 different expressions at a time'

Another reason for a more diverse drinking scene in the city is the growing enthusiasm for more eco-friendly wines among consumers. Over the last decade, Bordeaux vineyards have faced criticism for their high prices, conservatism, reliance on intensive farming practices and, in some cases, the excessive use of chemicals in the vineyards and additives in the cellars. This 'Bordeaux bashing' phenomenon explains why a new generation of sommeliers, bartenders and wine merchants in town increasingly look to showcase organic, biodynamic and even natural wines from many other regions of France.

Curious wine lovers lured to the city for its connection with wine will be pleased to learn that many top bars offer a vast selection of wine by the glass – Le Sobre, Le Bar à Vin du CIVB and Aux Quatre Coins du Vin, in particular – sometimes listing up to 40 different expressions at a time. And another positive characteristic of Bordeaux city's scene is that its bars are concentrated downtown, primarily in the St-Pierre or Chartrons neighbourhoods. Meaning that all of the best wine bars listed below are conveniently within walking distance of each other and primed for a vinous bar crawl.

Soif

35 Rue du Cancera

Tucked away down a small alley in the St-Pierre neighbourhood, Soif serves exquisite dishes and acts as a rendezvous spot for trendy chefs and wine personalities. And with good reason: the cellar boasts nearly 350 low-intervention wine selections. Expect top names, outsiders and the hard-to-find, from all corners of France and beyond: Bordeaux, the Dordogne, Champagne, Burgundy, the Loire, Savoie, Roussillon, Catalonia, the Douro... the list goes on. Don't miss exceptional bottles featuring rare grape varieties crafted by 'terroirist' Domaine Plageoles, whose estate is just a three-hour drive away.

www.soif-bordeaux.com

Soif

Where winemakers dine

A not-to-be missed restaurant in the Médoc is **Le Saint Julien** in Saint-Julien-Beychevelle. I really enjoy the traditional cuisine of this restaurant located on the Route des Châteaux du Médoc, which offers fresh and good-quality products and a fine wine list. Meanwhile, in the beautiful countryside of Sauternes, you'll find **l'Auberge les Vignes**, which is run by a very friendly team. It is one of the region's undiscovered treasures, with sublime food paired with great Sauternes. Moving back to the centre of Bordeaux, let me also recommend **Frida** – a cocktail bar, wine paradise and restaurant rolled into one. It offers a concise menu of sophisticated local dishes served in among a fun atmosphere. There is also a lovely garden for alfresco drinking in the warmer months. The wine selection, too, is impressive.

**Pierre Montégut,
Château Pichon Baron**

L'Univerre
40 Rue Lecocq

With more than 1,300 wines, this unassuming corner house is quite the standout. The list leans towards organic and biodynamic wines – but without being sectarian in its selection – and offers them at affordable prices. Traditional vintages mingle with prize wines from small producers, while fine wines sit alongside offerings from every region of France and beyond. The sommelier team delights in guiding customers with weekly glass selections, wines of the month, personal favourites and food-pairing suggestions (its no-fuss kitchen is focused on local produce). Just across the road, L'Univerre has also opened a grocery store and a cellar specializing in burgundy and boasting over 2,000 selections.

www.univerre-restaurant.com

Buvette pecorino

Le Sobre
24 Quai des Chartrons

Despite its contradictory name ('sobre' means 'sober' in French), this Chartrons wine bar and cellar offers a comprehensive selection of French appellations, along with a wide array of international bottles. Take your pick from the cellar shop and enjoy your chosen bottle on-site with a low corkage fee (an additional €10 per bottle). With around 25 wines available by the glass, there's also plenty to explore if just stopping by. Should you fancy flexing any newly acquired Bordeaux wine knowledge, there's even a blind tasting each week with a small prize awarded to the winner.

www.lesobrechartrons-bordeaux.fr/en

Buvette
41 Cours d'Alsace-et-Lorraine

Marianne Lay opened her cute wine bar and cellar in the St-Pierre neighbourhood in June 2022, its walls filled with wine bottles climbing four metres high. Aiming to make wine accessible, Buvette offers nearly 70 wines (natural, biodynamic and organic), with a rotating selection of wines by the glass (€5–6 per glass), including three reds, three whites, a rosé, plus a natural sparkling or orange wine. For a bottle, expect to pay an average of €25–30. You can also enjoy snacks on-site (cured meats, cheeseboards, small plates to share and piadinas), with tables placed out the front as soon as the sun is shining.

@buvette_bordeaux

Bacchus
5 Rue des Faussets

This brand-new restaurant not only offers dishes of excellent quality – refined and precise – but also boasts an eclectic selection of wines, its list featuring over 250 references. You can handpick bottles from a cellar that's right in the heart of the restaurant. Among them are many great reds from Bordeaux (Château Pichon Baron and Domaine de Chevalier among the star choices). Prices range from €43 for a 2019 Francs-Côtes-de-Bordeaux from Château Puygueraud to €322 for the 2012 St-Emilion Grand Cru from Château Figeac.

www.bacchus-bordeaux.fr

Le Sobre

CIVB wine bar

Le Bar à Vin du CIVB
3 Cours du 30 juillet

On the ground floor of an elegant 18th-century building combining neoclassical architecture with contemporary furnishings, this bar run by the Conseil Interprofessionnel des Vins de Bordeaux is ideal for sampling wines from the region without blowing your budget. You will find approximately 40 to 50 wines by the glass at rock-bottom prices. From a Bordeaux Supérieur for €2.50 to a Château Ladignac Cru Bourgeois 2011 for €3. The result is a unique atmosphere: tourists mingling with locals, novices with connoisseurs. As a bonus, the terrace overlooks the city's Grand Théâtre. A word of warning: in the evening, you might have to queue to get into this popular pitstop on a Bordeaux bar tour.

baravin.bordeaux.com

Aux Quatre Coins du Vin

8 Rue de la Devise

Just around the corner from the 15th-century St-Pierre church in the heart of Bordeaux, this sleek wine and charcuterie bar is a must-visit. It features dispensing machines that allow you to taste the wine you want in the measure you desire (30, 60 or 120ml). The wine list is neatly organized in a heavy leather binder, proudly showcasing over 1,800 wines, including 40 served by the glass that change regularly. Enjoy the top estates as well as wines from lesser-known producers, or delve in deeper at one of the bar's recently launched masterclasses – the first edition with Château Ausone and the second pouring from the likes of Cos d'Estournel.

@aux4coinsduvin

Au Bon Jaja

4 Cours d'Alsace-et-Lorraine

Even though 'jaja' (often used informally and humorously) means 'plonk' in French, you won't be finding low-quality wine here. Behind a storefront with pink neon lights, located just a few metres from the banks of the Garonne, this bar is the perfect place for adventurous souls and natural wine enthusiasts. The walls are adorned with bottles sorted by colour and region (featuring only organic, biodynamic or natural wines). Enjoy small dishes to share at very reasonable prices.

www.aubonjaja.fr

La Cave de la Gironde

36 Rue Moulinié

This is the kind of place that gets passed around by word of mouth. Opened in 2022 in this somewhat offbeat corner of Bordeaux – largely unknown to tourists – La Cave boasts around 300 wine selections; owner Thierry Basbayon has curated an astonishing range of reasonably priced wines. It's both a wine shop and bar (open Thursday to Saturday evenings), as well as an unpretentious bistro serving French dishes for sharing, such as roasted camembert, devilled eggs, cheese platters and sausages (open Tuesday to Friday lunchtimes). It looks like something straight out of a dreamy 1970s film set, complete with a Formica counter, chairs and stools. There's a large communal table in the centre of the room, accommodating up to a dozen guests.

www.cavedelagironde.com

Julo

Julo

11 Rue des Faures

A cozy wine bar with a lovely terrace overlooking the St-Michel Basilica. Savvy owner Julien Chivé (everyone here knows him by his nickname, 'Julo') offers up exclusive wines paired with delightful small plates. Blending elements of a wine shop, wine bar and gourmet grocery store, this spot offers over 700 wines from all regions of France. Expect to find drops from Bordeaux, but also the Rhône, Languedoc, Loire or Jura, all alongside a curated selection of international offerings. When it comes to the wines of Bordeaux, expect terroir-driven expressions from talented winemakers.

julobordeaux.wixsite.com/julo

Where winemakers dine

Lagrange has been a close friend of local restaurants and sommeliers for a long time. In the Médoc, **Le Saint Julien** restaurant is the best place to have a leisurely meal – expect seasonal ingredients prepared to a high standard, and an amazing wine list. Closer to Bordeaux, **Le Lion d'Or** in Arcins and the **Golf du Médoc** resort offer great food and wines. Of course, you'll find a plethora of choice in downtown Bordeaux, catering to a wide variety of preferences and budgets: **Ishikawa**, **Ganache**, **L'Univerre**, **TentaziOni**, **Maison Nouvelle**, **Le Mondrian** and **Gueuleton** are all at the top of their game. From *bistronomie* to *gastronomie*, from classical French cuisine to the best of Japanese food, you won't be disappointed. Particularly as every one of the above offers a wide selection of Bordeaux wines. But, most importantly of all, don't forget to add the finest brasserie in Bordeaux to your list: **Le Chiopot**.

**Matthieu Bordes,
Château Lagrange**

Staying in a Bordeaux château

Bordeaux has been enthusiastic about foreigners for a very long time – but usually as customers rather than guests. From at least the time of Eleanor of Aquitaine's marriage to the man who shortly afterwards ascended the English throne as Henry II, Bordelais ships would load up with local wine and sail north; when the two countries weren't warring (and when they were, Bordeaux was on the English side) visitors were welcome, but only the very privileged would be invited to stay. Recently, that has changed.

Château Bauduc

Wine lovers who have come all this way want more than a bottle and a bill; they want an experience, and the châteaux of Bordeaux, set amid the vines that spread from the Gironde estuary along the banks of the Garonne and Dordogne rivers, are well placed to provide just that. There is so much more than wine here, from the seafood and beaches of Arcachon to the beautiful historic cities of Bordeaux and St-Emilion. Not all the châteaux have become involved in tourism; good luck getting into Château Margaux, for example. But many, including several classed growths, have understood that the allure of a bottle of Bordeaux is as much about place as about flavour.

'This is the chance to be a château-dweller, at least briefly; to live a fantasy fuelled by fine wine'

There is no wine that cannot be enhanced by a memory of vines, good food, sunshine, relaxation and a lovely and unusual place to stay. A profound understanding of what makes Bordeaux great includes the chance to rub the gravel between your fingers, to taste looking over the vines. That, too, is terroir. For those who love history, it's a thrill to see the 18th-century Place de la Bourse in Bordeaux, where Mammon and Bacchus once met, or the imposing wall in St-Emilion that is all that remains of a 12th-century Dominican monastery. Sunseekers will enjoy a trip down one of the rivers or a day out beside the coast.

These days, it is also possible to book a room in an ancient château (radically repurposed to ensure that the medieval experience isn't too authentic); there are unusual options ranging from farmhouses to treehouses. This is the chance to be a château-dweller, at least briefly; to live a fantasy fuelled by fine wine. And planting oneself like a vine in the Bordeaux region also solves the wine tourist's biggest dilemma: how to see the sights and drink the wines without worrying about transport. This may be the greatest luxury of temporarily opting to call a château home.

La Maison d'Estournel, Château Cos d'Estournel, St-Estèphe

Louis Gaspard d'Estournel inherited this estate, now classed as a Second Growth, in 1791 and chose, daringly, to sail to India to sell his wines there himself. His admiration for that country is visible in the pagodas and elephants that decorate Château Cos d'Estournel and earned him the nickname 'the Maharajah of St-Estèphe', but he actually lived at Château Pomys down the road, in a mansion that hotelier Michel Reybier (who bought Cos in 2000) has now reunited with the rest of the estate and turned into a luxurious hotel. Fourteen rooms, tastefully decorated with just a touch of chintz, overlook the vineyards; there is a pool, a bistro restaurant with open kitchen, electric bikes to tour the vines and the opportunity to visit the château – with a special tasting specifically for hotel guests, in addition to vineyard tours, with or without lunch. And for those looking to get even closer to Cos, the owners' sumptuous eight-bedroom residence, a tower with indoor pool within the grounds that is known as La Chartreuse, is available to rent on an exclusive-use basis.

www.lamaison-estournel.com

Château Léognan, Léognan

This château opened as a hotel in 2023, with 17 plush, airy bedrooms plus five '*logements insolites*' or unusual accommodation options: three treehouses and two lodges, all facing the vines. There are 70 hectares of grounds, including six hectares of vines (Philippe Miecaze, who owns the property with his wife Chantal, is also the winemaker), a spa and Le Manège, the fine-dining restaurant, whose chef Gael Derrien trained at the George V and Shangri-La hotels in Paris. Derrien marries the sophistication he learned there with the simplicity of good ingredients, locally and seasonally sourced, including herbs from his own garden. There are plans for more restaurants and rooms and a heated pool in the former

Léognan

Bauduc

stables, but those won't be opening until 2026.

www.châteauleognan.com/en

The Farmhouse, Château Bauduc, Créon

Gavin and Angela Quinney are English, although they have been here in the Entre-Deux-Mers region since 1999, raising a family and making such good, well-priced wines that they have won praise, and more importantly space on the wine list, from top English restaurateurs including Rick Stein and Gordon Ramsay. Their accommodation is a four-bedroom farmhouse in the vineyard, with its own pool, a comfortable living area that has an open kitchen, wooden beams and a fireplace. The Quinneys have lots of recommendations for places to pick up good ingredients in Créon, the

Where winemakers dine

I can heartily recommend **L'Envers du Décor** in St-Emilion and **Le Caffé Cuisine** in Branne – the latter is on the Left Bank of the Dordogne. These two restaurants offer delicious homemade cuisine, made with fresh and local produce. The atmosphere, too, is very friendly and welcoming in both venues, while the wine lists sparkle with creativity and passion. It is hard to imagine two nicer places to have lunch while exploring the region, in the heart of the legendary village of St-Emilion or on the banks of the Dordogne.

Philippe Chandon-Moët, Château de Ferrand

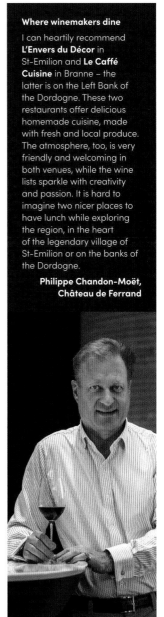

14th-century town that is walking distance down the road, including the Wednesday market; they are happy to offer guided vineyard walks, winery tours and tastings, or guests can just wander around on their own. And if all that rural peace gets too much, the bright lights of Bordeaux are just 40 minutes' drive away.

www.bauduc.com

Château Pape Clément, Pessac

When Bernard de Goth became Pope in 1305 and took the name Clement V, his family had already been tending vines at the property now named after him for half a century. There is nothing medieval about the current château, though, not even the magnificently turreted walls; it was rebuilt in 1864. And certainly not the facilities, which include large, light bedrooms and vast gardens dotted with artworks and botanical curiosities such as a thousand-year-old olive tree and a Cedar of Lebanon planted before the French Revolution. Truffles from the four truffle oaks owned by proprietor Bernard Magrez elevate a restaurant that is already special, and a stay here can include a visit of the Grand Cru Classé estate and wine tastings in various formats, including a cheese-pairing

workshop. Despite its lovely grounds, the château is almost in Bordeaux, with the Quai des Chartrons less than 10km away.

www.château-pape-clement.fr/en

Château Lafaurie-Peyraguey, Sauternes

The Lalique hotel collection, like the crystal objects that made René Lalique famous, is small but perfectly formed; Glenturret in Scotland and three establishments in France, including this fairytale castle with 18 hectares of enclosed vineyard in Sauternes, the region that is home to the world's greatest sweet wine. The château has 10 bedrooms and three suites with views over vineyards that have been cultivated since 1618; the restaurant boasts two Michelin stars and a 350,000-bottle

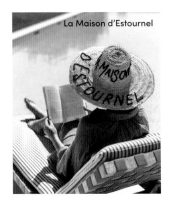

La Maison d'Estournel

cellar including all the top Bordeaux wines, red, white and sweet. Both are decorated with interiors, chandeliers and art in the exquisite Art Deco style that Lalique perfected in the 1920s. Tours and tastings are available by appointment and the excitements of Bordeaux are just 45 minutes' drive – if you can wrench yourself away.

www.lafauriepeyragueylalique.com/en/the-domain/château

Hôtel de Pavie

Hôtel de Pavie, Château Pavie, St-Emilion

There may be no better place to admire the white walls of St-Emilion than the large terrace at the Hôtel de Pavie, formerly known as the Hostellerie de Plaisance. This hotel and restaurant in the UNESCO World Heritage-listed city on Bordeaux's Right Bank has been under the aegis of the Perse family, owners of Premier Grand Cru Classé estate Château de Pavie, since 2001. These days, the restaurant is under the direction of Yannick Alléno and has two Michelin stars, and there are 22 rooms and suites, decorated in a bright contemporary style, in a trio of buildings. One of these is La Maison de Clocher, next to the bell tower of the famous monolithic church. The 68-m tower is the only part above ground; the body of the church was dug out of the limestone in the early 12th century. The wine estate is a pleasant 25-minute walk away and visits must be booked, although the wines can of course be enjoyed with Alléno's superb food as well.

www.hoteldepavie.com/en

The Keys, Château Troplong Mondot, St-Emilion

The nearby water tower signals that this is the highest hill in the area, although the gorgeous views from the gracious mansion across the vineyards to St-Emilion may already have given that away. It's a lovely 25-minute walk to town, too, sometimes passing one of the horses used to work the vineyards' soil. Amid the vines stands the two-bedroom Vineyard House, with its chequered floor and open fire, and there is also The Keys, next door to the château, which incorporates two bedrooms and a two-bedroom suite, the Art Studio, once used by Christine Valette-Pariente, the estate's owner until her death in 2014. Each can be booked separately, and the pool outside the main house is open to all guests. David Charrier's restaurant Les Belles Perdrix holds a Michelin star – and if there were stars for beautiful views, its vast windows overlooking the vines would have earned one of those as well.

www.troplong-mondot.com/en

Cordeillan-Bages

Château Cordeillan-Bages, Bages

Jean-Michel Cazes died in 2023 aged 88, and the obituaries made clear that he had fit so much achievement into his life that even those many decades don't seem enough for all he accomplished. Putting Pauillac, then a backwater uninterested in (and unprepared for) visitors, firmly on the tourism map was an important part of that. In addition to modernizing Château Lynch-Bages and Ormes de Pez – the two estates his grandfather bought – he added others, renovated the whole village of Bages and founded this beautiful 28-room hotel. Situated in a 19th-century building of creamy Bordeaux stone that still retains traces of its 17th-century predecessor, it is filled with works of art and designer furniture and is, of course, surrounded by vines. For a long time, there was a Michelin-starred restaurant in-house; these days, dining is a few steps away at Café Lavinal in the village, but the heated pool, gym and sauna are still very much on offer, as are vineyard tours.

www.cordeillanbages.com/en/hotel

Where to eat and drink in St-Emilion

St-Emilion is so utterly different to the city of Bordeaux that it takes the traveller completely by surprise. This UNESCO World Heritage Site, a centuries-old stop on the pilgrim route, its steep cobbled streets leading onto medieval squares and ancient monuments, is one of Bordeaux's most-visited towns.

La Table de Pavie

Key to St-Emilion's charms is the fact that – ancient though it may be, and visited by over a million tourists a year – it's very much a living, working town. It's entirely surrounded by vineyards (some producing the world's most renowned and expensive wines), and almost all of its 2,500 residents are directly connected to the wine business that has thrived here for centuries.

According to legend, St-Emilion's story began around 750 CE. Emilion, a monk from Brittany, settled in a cave that became his hermitage, and was joined by an evangelical band of disciples. After his death, they continued his work; a church was carved into the rocky limestone block. You can still admire this true underground sanctuary that dates back to the early 12th century and against which the Pavie hotel is nestled.

During the Middle Ages, the village developed around this historical cave. The Hundred Years' War passed through St-Emilion, during which time the town regularly changed flags as English and French authorities fought for control of the city. And by the 16th century, the Wars of Religion weakened the medieval town, quickly reducing it to the size of a small village. The rediscovery of this fabulous terroir didn't happen until the second half of the 18th century and into the 19th century, when legendary estates such as Château Ausone, Château Cheval Blanc and Château Angelus brought a new prosperity to the region, recognized as an AOC in 1936. With the success of these vineyards came the creation of an impressive number of hotels, guesthouses, wine shops and guided tours.

Since the pandemic, there have been various renovation projects and the establishment of new businesses. The Pavie Hotel is now expanding with five new suites in the village, all nestled within an old 16th-century wine merchant's house; Le Glacier is a purveyor of frozen creations such as basil and tomato sorbet (crafted by the pastry chef of La Table de Pavie) on one of St-Emilion's most famous streets, rue du Clocher, next to bistro L'Envers du Décor.

But St-Emilion isn't the city of Bordeaux: don't expect avant-garde cuisine. Even if talented chefs like triple-starred Yannick Alléno – who wants to *'bring Bordeaux cuisine out of its bourgeois spirit'* – have put down roots or opened up restaurants in the area, the dining and drinking scene in St-Emilion remains rooted in terroir and tradition.

Read on for a selection of eight top restaurants and bars in St-Emilion. To avoid disappointment, advance bookings are recommended, especially in the summer months.

Le Cloître des Cordeliers
2 Rue de la Porte Brunet

Stroll through the serene cloister leading to the garden of a former convent. This 13th-century monastery, classified as a historical monument, has been transformed in part into an elegant wine bar. While you could indulge in a glass of the red that permeates the region, something local and sparkling is surprisingly what's suggested here. This is where Crémant de Bordeaux is crafted, in caves stretching 3km-long and 17m underground – which are also available to explore on a guided tour. There's a sleek multi-storey boutique adjacent to the action and offering a selection of regional products, enhancing the charm of this delightful spot.

www.lescordeliers.com

La Table de Pavie
5 Place du Clocher

Star chef Yannick Alléno took over the kitchens of the Pavie hotel in 2020. The restaurant currently holds two Michelin stars and is now aiming for its coveted third. Standout dishes on a recent visit included poached langoustine with vanilla seed, with a stew of the heads in Esprit de Pavie wine, or the roasted pigeon, with ortolan-style beak, breast with bitter sorrel jus and a walnut purée – without giving too much of a spoiler, it's a spectacular nod to the (now-outlawed) French ritual of ortolan eating. Extensive and impressive, the wine list offers a splendid selection of the region's finest appellations.

www.hoteldepavie.com/la-table-de-pavie.html

Where winemakers dine

I have a strong preference today for **Le 1925**, situated at the heart of Bordeaux's downtown area. Indeed, despite the fact that there are many restaurants to choose from in Bordeaux, 1925 pips them to the post. But why? It is partly because the city had previously been lacking a champion of classical food in a traditional brasserie setting. It has the atmosphere of *les années folles* [1920s France] in the heart of Bordeaux. Moreover, the amazing wine list represents more than 600 wines chosen by owner Pierre Martin, a wine lover who also discovered many small wineries in different areas in France. I'm also very fond of **Le Chapon Fin**, which serves excellent food in a refined atmosphere featuring luxurious décor. The **Hôtel & Restaurant Le Saint-James** is another excellent choice: good food and superb views of Bordeaux city.

**Claire Villars-Lurton,
G&C Lurton Estates
(Château Durfort-Vivens,
Château Ferrière, Château
Haut-Bages Libéral,
Château La Gurgue)**

Café Saigon
21 Rue Guadet

In St-Emilion, anything is possible: even eating shrimp spring rolls while sipping on a Château Angelus 2010. In the heart of the village, this brilliant Asian canteen is run by a Franco-Vietnamese duo. Keep it simple with a shrimp salad, red cabbage and fresh coriander, or opt for succulent pork and mushroom dumplings. All the finest French vintages are here: Clos de la Maréchale 2016 by Jacques-Frédéric Mugnier (€165), Vosne-Romanée 2016 by Emmanuel Rouget (€500)... even La Tâche 2018 from Domaine de la Romanée-Conti (€2,900). They also offer wines by the glass (€5–9) and more affordable bottles, such as the Rhône Valley's Les Tours 2016 by Emmanuel Reynaud (€38).

www.facebook.com/
cafesaigon33330

Sous la Robe
21 Rue André Loiseau

The sommelier-owner of Sous la Robe wine bar offers impeccable guidance on French wine and champagne, on the list here at a reasonable price. Whether you're seated inside the rustic bar or out on its terrace, a delightful selection of cheese, foie gras and charcuterie also awaits. Plus, the bar's new kitchen

Sous la Robe

should open soon, and artistic and musical performances are now taking place in their basement, which previously housed an underground museum.

www.facebook.com/
souslarobesaintemilion

Logis de la Cadène
3 Place du Marché au Bois

Founded in 1848 and acquired since by the prestigious Château Angelus, this one-star Michelin restaurant is the oldest in St-Emilion. Guests are charmed by its ancient golden stonework and wisteria trained up the terrace's pergola. Arriving in September 2023, new chef Thibaut Gamba offers refined and delicate plates, prioritizing the use of local Aquitaine products to the fullest. Some of the fruit and vegetables that feature come from the estate's farm, as does the honey. The wine list features several hundred vintages from some of the world's finest vineyards, including the owner Château Angelus. If you want to indulge and leave the driving for tomorrow, the venue also doubles as an intimate hotel.

www.logisdelacadene.fr/en

L'Envers du Décor
11 Rue du Clocher

You can't miss the bright red façade of this wine bar-bistro, just a stone's throw from the Tourist Office. On the menu at St-Emilion's oldest wine bar? French market cuisine focusing on local producers. Think slow-cooked lamb shoulder or a rib of beef to share between

Grand Barrail

is done with respect for the natural environment in mind. Chef David Charrier relies on perfectly mastered techniques and offers a hyper-local cuisine, favouring products from the estate and from rigorously selected small producers. The wine list is all about indulgence without breaking the bank.

www.troplong-mondot.com/en

Château Grand Barrail
Route de Libourne D243

Antique mouldings, exceptional stained-glass windows and Oriental-style paintings at this hotel make for an effect reminiscent of the work of architect 'Viollet-le-Duc'. Built in 1902, this elegant château blends the old with contemporary design. At lunch in its restaurant, enjoy bistro-style dishes like roasted aubergine with smoked caviar, tomato sauce and fig-infused balsamic. Dinner offers more ambitious options such as Charolais beef tenderloin with bread-sauce, truffle and cabbage. You can sit in either the Art Nouveau-inspired lounge or on the beautiful terrace overlooking the estate and a sea of vines. As a bonus, the estate's wine bar is typically open from June until September, from 5pm to 11pm.

www.grand-barrail.com/en/restaurant

two, plus Grand Marnier soufflé to finish. A fine wine list (with 500 references, and not just Bordeaux) offers reasonable prices, with a wide selection available by the glass. L'Envers du Décor boasts the added advantage of a lovely sunny terrace, making it the perfect spot for a leisurely lunch (and a digestif).

www.envers-dudecor.com

Les Belles Perdrix de Troplong Mondot
Château Troplong Mondot

Located atop a small hill (the highest point of St-Emilion), this Michelin-starred restaurant with sleek dining room is a must-visit. The huge bay window, stretching towards the horizon, opens onto the magnificent Troplong Mondot vineyard. Here, biodiversity is a priority, and everything

Five of the best Bordeaux wine shops

Prince Robert of Luxembourg has opened a smart new wine shop in the centre of Bordeaux, but it's only one among many excellent modern boutiques in the wine world's most historic city. Here we list five of the best.

Au Bon Jaja

In a city where négociants have traditionally held sway, Bordeaux's wine merchants have tended to service clients around the world and through the somewhat opaque sale of *en primeur* wines buried deep in their bonded warehouses. But there's a rising scene of Bordeaux wine boutiques tapping into the increasing number of visitors drawn to a city famous for its wine – and perhaps hoping for a little souvenir to take away from their visit.

As a collector himself – of medieval art, recipe books and eclectic curios – Prince Robert of Luxembourg, owner of Domaine Clarence Dillon (which counts Château Haut-Brion and La Mission Haut-Brion among its holdings), knows this audience well. He details how one question lay central to the opening of the group's original wine shop, La Cave du Château in Paris: 'At the end of the day, how do we produce something that will attract even ourselves?' he says. Tapping into the psyche of his fellow collectors, he and the team were able to flesh out a list of desirable wines from across France to populate the boutique's smart shelves. It's a formula that's been successful enough to spawn a second shop at the château's visitor centre and a third in the heart of the city, which opened on the Place de Tourny in 2024.

L'Intendant

It's not the only wine shop in Bordeaux that defers to other regions despite the illustrious location. The logic follows that Bordeaux visitors and residents alike are sure to have a love of fine wine that doesn't just stay loyal to the local. Should you be less tied to the idea of snapping up a *grand vin* for the cellar, the city's passion for all kinds of wine can be witnessed at shops like Au Bon Jaja, which doubles as a bar and throngs with life after hours, altogether going against the preconceptions of Bordeaux as a stuffy, old-school wine city.

And while the small matter of strict allocations on the latest releases might make the classed growth wines hard to come by, there are some strong exceptions for shopping in Bordeaux. Look for places that are able to work their contact book. For example, L'Intendant, opposite the Grand Théâtre, is owned by one of the city's leading négociants, which boasts connections with 500 Bordeaux châteaux including a number of Grand Cru properties. If you want to increase your chances of getting a hand on some of the region's most desired labels further still, many of these wine boutiques foster relationships with customers through in-store events, including tastings with the makers. Get on their books, and who knows what the inside track might offer?

Five top wine shops in Bordeaux city

La Cave du Château: Bordeaux
3 Place de Tourny

Opening its doors in 2024 on the Place de Tourny, La Cave du Château is a spin-off from the physical Paris shop and online e-store and shares the bold aim of becoming 'one of the finest retailers in France', according to its owner Prince Robert of Luxembourg. It boasts 800 references, from wines for the everyday to small hidden gems – mostly hailing from within France, with just a few exceptions. At the entrance, there's muted décor that allows the rows of bottles from across the country to do the talking, with Burgundy and Bordeaux tucked to the rear – although currently its store managers say they get more enquiries for Jura than for Burgundy. Loyal customers are promised access to deals that won't be found online (with the shop's Haut-Brion connection, it might be a worthwhile pursuit), and there's an aim for the space to be put to use for client events and premium tastings by reservation. Plus, come the summer, the shop hopes to add tables to its terrace on the attractive roundabout for customers to enjoy a glass.

www.lacaveduchâteau.com

L'Intendant
2 Allées de Tourny

The provenance of bottles from the top châteaux is assured at L'Intendant thanks to the shop's ownership; Duclot is one of Bordeaux's oldest négociants and its holding company also owns Pétrus (and Badie, below). With its connections and its history, you can expect to find the likes of Lafite and Latour on the shelves. Indeed, L'Intendant has a library of 1,600 labels and a heavy focus on the wines of the region; its references include those higher up the classification system as well as producers from smaller appellations. A sweeping spiral staircase encased in bottle-lined shelves is often the star of social media posts, but take the journey in real life to be led up the scale of prestige, with large format and hard-to-find vintages reserved for the top, five storeys up.

www.intendant.com

Badie
60-62 Allées de Tourny

The address on Allées de Tourny has a historic reputation as a pioneering Bordeaux wine merchant, first opened by Madame Badie in 1880. Now part of the mighty Duclot empire, with 3,500 labels it has twice the range of its sister shop L'Intendant (above). The champagne selection is

Badie

first-rate (Badie also makes a house bubbly), and every other region of France, from the Loire to the Jura, is amply covered: there's a huge selection from Burgundy and Rhône, for example. Apart from a wealth of whiskies and other spirits, there's even a decent wine offering from the rest of the world (though generally only the most exalted bottles). The sommelier team runs regular evening masterclasses covering everything from tequila and mezcal to the Loire and Languedoc-Roussillon.

www.badie.com

Au Bon Jaja
4 Cours d'Alsace-et-Lorraine

Its charming summer terrace by day and its neon-lit interior by night might draw in plenty of thirsty visitors to Au Bon Jaja for a glass of wine, but this hybrid Bordeaux destination is just as deserving of a shopping trip as it is a drinking session. This vibrant bar and shop just up from the banks of the Garonne champions biodynamic and organic wine – and the best part is you can try before you commit to buying a whole bottle. Colourful labels line the shelves, unpretentious staff are on hand for guidance and the selection of bottles offers a window into some of the emerging winemaking trends currently sweeping the country, with a strong selection from the Loire and Burgundy to boot.

www.aubonjaja.fr

Max Bordeaux
14 Cours de l'Intendance

Maximum pleasure is on the agenda at Max Bordeaux in the Triangle d'Or, signalled by its decorative ceiling installation of inverted wine glasses and its prominent Enomatic machines on the shop floor. The hybrid venue doubles as a tasting space (or 'wine gallery', in its own words) where popular masterclasses can be arranged for visiting groups and where trying by the glass is encouraged during browsing sessions; but rest assured that you can take a bottle or case away with you after a visit. Some 45 famous Crus are represented: from Margaux to Cheval Blanc, d'Yquem, Smith Haut Lafitte, Domaine de Chevalier... The *caviste* calls itself a Grand Cru specialist with an aim to make these sought-after wines far more accessible.

www.maxbordeaux.com

La Cave du Château

L'Intendant

Bordeaux's greatest wines

A list of Bordeaux's 'greatest' wines is necessarily subjective. A wine critic might base his or her list on scores and tasting notes alone. For a wine merchant, prestige and price are major factors; an investor sets most store by the wine's value in the secondary, or auction, market.

Reputations rise and fall, but as we've seen (in Bordeaux's classification systems, pages 28–33) the list of most-renowned, and most bankable, châteaux has remained pretty steady over the last 150 years. Generally speaking, there are a dozen or so properties on the Left and Right Banks that might be considered 'Bordeaux's Greatest Wines': wines that are highly sought-after by collectors and investors for their consistency, complexity and ageing potential.

Left Bank

Château Haut-Brion, Premier Cru Classé de Graves. An innovative estate with the oldest history of viticulture of the First Growths (it is famously mentioned by Samuel Pepys, the great 17th-century diarist). Just 5km away from Bordeaux city, Haut-Brion makes red and white wines with both a *grand vin* (first wine) and second wine, Le Clarence de Haut-Brion, made from young vines. The two white wines are Haut-Brion Blanc and La Clarté de Haut-Brion, taking grapes from both the estate and sister property La Mission Haut-Brion.

Haut-Brion was bought in 1935 by Domaine Clarence Dillon. The aim was to restore the estate to its former glory, and reclaim its place in the elite circle of the world's most legendary wines. It was among the first in the region to introduce stainless steel vats for winemaking and is routinely among the first to harvest grapes given its close proximity to the city of Bordeaux with its complexity of warm soils ranging from limestone to large gravels and deep clays.

The *grand vin* blend typically includes more Merlot than the other four First Growths. It displays incredible robustness and aromatic intensity especially as it ages, as well as distinctive minerality and overall refinement. The family business, chaired by Prince Robert of Luxembourg, also owns La Mission Haut-Brion and Quintus (St-Emilion).

La Mission Haut-Brion, Cru Classé de Graves, Pessac-Léognan. Linked to Haut-Brion since the mid-16th century (the two are neighbours) but not under the same ownership until 1983. Both estates are run with their own identities but under the same winemaking teams.

The 30-hectare property, with 10% dedicated to white grapes, makes a red and white *grand vin* as well as a second red wine, La Chapelle de la Mission Haut-Brion and a second white wine, La Clarté. Soils are mainly gravel on a sub-strata of clay, sand and limestone with fairly equal plantings of Cabernet Sauvignon and Merlot and 10% of Cabernet Franc. The wines tend to be a little bit more full bodied, concentrated and upfront than Haut-Brion but with beautifully pure and poised aromatics.

If the 1855 classification were to be redrawn today, it's highly likely this estate would be awarded First Growth status.

La Mission Haut-Brion

Lafite Rothschild, Premier Grand Cru Classé, Pauillac. Arguably the greatest of the First Growths, with an iconic status within the global luxury goods market. Like Mouton it's owned by the Rothschilds, though different branches of the family tree. Domaines Barons de Rothschild has controlled Lafite since it was bought by James Rothschild in 1868. It's run today by sixth-generation millennial Saskia de Rothschild. The second wine is Carruades de Lafite, based on specific plots and strict selections.

The richly biodiverse and sustainably run vineyards lie on a high plateau and are planted on deep gravel to a majority of Cabernet Sauvignon; the *grand vin* comprises over 80% of these vineyards. It is generally less demonstrative and powerful than its Pauillac counterparts, focusing on nuance and elegance as well as a great ability to age.

The estate also owns Duhart-Milon (Pauillac), L'Evangile (Pomerol) and Rieussec (Sauternes).

Château Latour, Premier Grand Cru Classé, Pauillac. Latour has a long and venerable history; it's one of the most dynamic and precision-focused wineries in Bordeaux, with a focus on sustainable and biodynamic farming.

At 92 hectares, with a 47-hectare parcel, known as L'Enclos, surrounding the château, Latour produces three wines: the *grand vin*, second wine Les Forts de Latour and a third wine, Pauillac de Latour. Soils are sticky clay covered in well-draining gravel, giving the wines power and structure with exceptional freshness. They usually take longer to come around than the other Firsts – i.e. they're a bit serious and strict when young – but have remarkably consistent quality across vintages. Cabernet Sauvignon forms the majority of plantings and is the base of the blend at around or above 90%.

Latour famously left the *en primeur* system after the 2011 vintage in response to the increasing desire of consumers for ready-to-drink wines that have been stored in optimal conditions. It has a vast, purpose-built cellar full of not yet released wines.

The property is owned by French billionaire François Pinault, the chairman and CEO of luxury fashion group Kering (Gucci, Balenciaga, Yves Saint Laurent) and president of wine investment company Artémis Domaines. Also part of the group are Châteaux Siaurac (Lalande-de-Pomerol), Vray Croix de Gay (Pomerol) and Le Prieuré (St-Emilion). The company also owns estates in Napa Valley, the Rhône, Champagne and Burgundy.

Mouton Rothschild, Premier Grand Cru Classé, Pauillac.

Owned and run by fifth-generation members of the Rothschild dynasty. Bought by Nathaniel Rothschild in 1853, it is run today by Philippe Sereys de Rothschild, Julien de Beaumarchais de Rothschild and Camille Sereys de Rothschild. It is one of only two estates in the Médoc to remain in the same family since the 1855 classification.

Mouton is the most consciously aesthetic of the First Growths: since the 1940s it has commissioned artists – from Andy Warhol to Chagall, Braque, Picasso, Francis Bacon, Miró, the then Prince (now King) Charles, Dalí, Henry Moore, Jeff Koons – for its labels. It sits on gravel soils, well-suited to Cabernet Sauvignon, on a plateaued outcrop it shares with Lafite. Its second wine is Petit Mouton and there's a white, Aile d'Argent. Mouton's *grand vin* is renowned for its opulence of fruit flavours combined with silky textures, supple tannins and impressive length.

D'Armailhac (Pauillac) and Clerc Milon (Pauillac) are also in the family's Bordeaux holdings, as well as the long-established entry-level Mouton Cadet, which sources grapes from across the region.

Margaux, Premier Grand Cru Classé, Margaux.

Dating back to the 12th century, the estate is one of the oldest in the region, with a reputation for producing exceptional wines since the 18th century. It has been owned by the Mentzelopoulos family since the mid-20th century. The family invested heavily, modernized facilities and brought in organic vineyard practices. Château Margaux has been managed by successive generations of the family which now include siblings Alexis Leven-Mentzelopoulos and Alexandra Petit-Mentzelopoulos.

The estate produces three red wines: the *grand vin*, Pavillon Rouge and Margaux du Château Margaux; and two white wines, Pavillon Blanc and Pavillon Blanc Second Vin (starting from the 2022 vintage) made from 12 hectares of Sauvignon Blanc. Set on deep gravel soils, Margaux's wines are renowned for their delicate elegance and refined, highly perfumed aromatic profile with a fine balance of fruit, tannins and acidity.

It is the only one of the Firsts which has no sister estates, either in Bordeaux or elsewhere.

Other Left Bank wines with great reputations:

Châteaux Palmer (Third Growth Margaux), Léoville Las Cases and Ducru-Beaucaillou (Second Growths St-Julien), Cos d'Estournel (Second Growth St-Estèphe), Pichon Longueville and Pichon Baron (Second Growths Pauillac).

Pichon Baron

Right Bank

Cheval Blanc, St-Emilion Grand Cru. St-Emilion's most renowned estate, the LVMH-owned Cheval Blanc left the St-Emilion classification with the 2022 vintage, dropping the Premier Grand Cru Classé designation from its labels.

Arguably one of the most famous wines in the world, Cheval has had a historic reputation for excellence since the 16th century. Over the years, the estate has been owned by several prominent families and individuals each contributing to its legacy and reputation as one of Bordeaux's finest wine producers.

Today, it is owned by the Frère family and luxury goods company LVMH. Celebrated for its terroir, which includes a unique combination of well-draining Pomerol-esque clay planted to Cabernet Franc, and gravel planted to Merlot; roughly a fifth of its soils are typical St-Emilion terroir of sandy soils over a limestone bedrock. At only 39 hectares it is much smaller than many Left Bank estates, which contributes greatly to its exclusivity. The estate generally makes a large proportion of *grand vin* at more than 70% with 25% going to a second wine, Petit Cheval (there's also a white wine of the same name).

The estate has two sister sites in St-Emilion: Quinault l'Enclos and La Tour du Pin. LVMH also owns the Sauternes First Growth Château d'Yquem.

Ausone, St-Emilion Grand Cru. This estate was also recognized as one of the best estates in 1958, and also chose to remove itself from the recent classification. Owned by the Vauthier family, it's one of the most historic of all Bordeaux wines, with evidence of winemaking dating back to Roman times. It also commands some of the highest prices in Bordeaux. It farms only 7 hectares of vineyards; Ausone is in extremely high demand, particularly in the auction market, which makes the wines more likely to be traded and stored than opened and enjoyed.

Cheval Blanc

The estate is perched on a limestone plateau above the village of St-Emilion. The vines are organically farmed, planted on steep slopes with a majority of Cabernet Franc and Merlot and smaller percentages of Cabernet Sauvignon and Petit Verdot. Almost all the production goes into the *grand vin*, with 10% going into the second wine, La Chapelle d'Ausone.

The family also owns de Fontbel, La Clotte, Moulin St-Georges, Simard and Haut-Simard in St-Emilion.

Pétrus, Pomerol. Pétrus is one of the world's iconic wines. It is celebrated for its unique position on the Pomerol plateau, its 11.5 hectares sitting on the famous blue clay of Pomerol, a sticky, iron-rich soil, 40 million years old. Pétrus is made only of Merlot.

There is no official second wine here with almost all production going into the *grand vin*. The Moueix family, specifically Jean-François and his son Jean, owns 80% of Pétrus with US-Colombian billionaire Alejandro Santo Domingo acquiring a minority 20% stake in 2018. The deal is said to have valued Pétrus at €1 billion which makes it the most expensive vineyard transaction on record.

Given the price and demand on the secondary market, you're more likely to see bottles in cellars than on tables.

Le Pin, Pomerol. A tiny, cultish estate with a short history but a reputation as one of the most in-demand wines in the region. It was founded in 1979 by the Belgian winemaker Jacques Thienpont, who recognized the potential of the 2.7-hectare vineyard to produce exceptional wines. Alexandre Thienpont of Vieux Château Certan has a minority stake and works as estate manager alongside his son Guillaume.

Le Pin is located on one of the highest sectors of the Pomerol plateau with neighbouring estates Vieux Château Certan, Petit-Village and Trotanoy. It is planted with 100% Merlot on essentially gravel soils with patches of sand and clay on an iron-rich base, with organically farmed vines averaging 40 years old.

Made in extremely limited quantities, and in some vintages not at all, Le Pin is an opulent, perfumed, concentrated wine with great complexity.

Angelus

Other Right Bank wines with great reputations:

Pavie (St-Emilion Grand Cru Classé A), Angelus (St-Emilion, left the classification in 2022); Figeac (St-Emilion Grand Cru Classé A); Lafleur (Pomerol), Trotanoy (Pomerol).

Lafite

Glossary

1855 Classification – the ranking created by Napoleon III for the 1855 World's Fair in Paris to showcase the best French wines, still of major relevance

Acidity – an essential component of wine, providing freshness and balance

AOC (Appellation d'Origine Contrôlée) – the French certification granted to certain wines, based on geographical location and adherence to traditional practices

Appellation – a legally defined geographical area used to identify where grapes for a wine were grown

Barrique – a 225-litre barrel most often (in Bordeaux) of French oak

Barsac – appellation neighbouring Sauternes, its wines often with a slightly lighter profile

Blaye – Right Bank appellation producing both red and white wines

Bordeaux Privilege – a historical trading right that restricted wine exports from the Bordeaux region before St Martin's Day (11 November)

Botrytis Cinerea – the fungus responsible for noble rot, crucial in the production of sweet wines like those from Sauternes

Cabernet Sauvignon – a prominent red grape variety in Bordeaux, valued for its structure, tannins and ageing potential

Cave – cellar used for ageing and storing wine, often associated with Bordeaux's historic estates

Cépage – grape variety; in Bordeaux, it typically refers to the mix of varieties used in the region's blends

Château – vineyard estate often with a grand manor house

Claret – traditional British term for red Bordeaux wine, derived from *clairet*, a light red wine

Côtes de Bordeaux – appellations along Bordeaux's Right Bank, known for affordable red wines

Côtes de Bourg – a Right Bank appellation known for producing fruity, approachable red wines

Courtier – wine broker, intermediary between château and négociant, a crucial cog in *La Place de Bordeaux*

Cru Classé – a wine listed in the 1855 Classification

Cuvée – a specific blend of wine, often from different grape varieties, vineyards or vintages

Eau-de-vie – distillation from wine or fermented fruit juice, historically significant in Bordeaux

En Primeur – a term for both the tasting and sale of wines that are still in barrel. Wines are assessed in the April following harvest and sold in a structured campaign usually beginning in May or June

Entre-Deux-Mers – large appellation between the Garonne and Dordogne rivers, known for its crisp dry white wines

First Growth – (see Premier Cru Classé)

Fronsac – lesser-known Right Bank appellation, producing robust, Merlot-dominated wines with good value and ageing potential

Garonne – Bordeaux's major river

Gironde Estuary – the waterway formed by the confluence of the Garonne and Dordogne rivers

Graves – a Left Bank appellation with a distinctive gravel terroir, producing both red and white wines

Haut-Médoc – a sub-region within Médoc containing prestigious appellations such as Margaux and St-Julien

Lalande-de-Pomerol – appellation adjacent to Pomerol, with Merlot-based wines

La Place de Bordeaux – historic virtual marketplace in which wine is traded through *courtiers* and négociants rather than directly to consumers; it plays a crucial role in the global distribution of Bordeaux wines

Left Bank – the western side of the Gironde estuary and Garonne River, known for Cabernet Sauvignon-dominated wines

Libournais – the collective term for the Right Bank wine regions surrounding the town of Libourne, including St-Emilion and Pomerol

Margaux – renowned appellation in Haut-Médoc, its wines often described as the most refined of Bordeaux

Médoc – an appellation on Bordeaux's Left Bank with some of the region's most famous properties

Merlot – an important red grape variety in Bordeaux, known for producing soft, approachable wines with ripe fruit flavours

Microclimate – the specific climatic conditions in a small, contained area

Muscadelle – lesser-known white grape variety often blended with Sauvignon Blanc and Sémillon

Négociant – wine merchant; often buys wine in bulk to age, blend, bottle and sell under own label; a key player in the global Bordeaux trade

Noble Rot – a beneficial fungus, *botrytis cinerea*, that dehydrates grapes, concentrating their sugars and flavours for sweet wine production

Pauillac – Left Bank appellation, famous for powerful, tannic red wines, including three of Bordeaux's five First Growths

Pessac-Léognan – sub-appellation of Graves, known for its exceptional red and white wines, including some of Bordeaux's finest white wines

Pomerol – small Right Bank appellation, renowned for some of Bordeaux's most opulent and luxurious Merlot-based wines

Premier Cru Classé (or First Growth) – top tier of the 1855 Classification

Right Bank – the eastern side of the Gironde estuary and Dordogne River, known for Merlot-dominated wines

Sauternes – appellation in Graves famous for its sweet white wines made from grapes affected by noble rot

Sauvignon Blanc – important white grape variety known for its crisp acidity and aromatic qualities

Sémillon – white grape variety used particularly in sweet wines and in some dry white blends

St-Emilion – Right Bank appellation, renowned for its Merlot-dominant wines

St-Estèphe – northernmost Médoc appellation, known for its full-bodied, tannic red wines with significant ageing potential

St-Julien – appellation in Haut-Médoc known for its harmonious and refined red wines

Tannin – a natural compound in wine, derived from grape skins, seeds and oak, that contributes to its structure and ageing potential

Terroir – the combination of natural factors such as soil, climate and topography that influence the characteristics of wine from a specific location

Tonneau – traditional unit of measure for wine volume, a barrel holding 900 litres

Vinification – the process of converting grapes into wine, including fermentation, ageing and bottling

Further reading

Bordeaux has attracted many great writers over the centuries, each bringing a unique perspective to its wine culture. This is a selection of histories, biographies, reference books and culinary works that should be on the shelf of oenophiles and enthusiasts – and those starting out on their Bordeaux journey.

History

1855: A History of The Bordeaux Classification by Dewey Markham
John Wiley & Sons, 1997
An exploration of the origins and implications of the 1855 classification

Wine and War by Don and Petie Kladstrup
Hodder, 2002
A fascinating account of how France's vintners protected their wine from Nazi plunder during World War II

Knee Deep in Claret: A Celebration of Wine and Scotland by Billy Kay and Cailean Maclean
Auld Alliance Publishing, 1994
A celebration of the deep-rooted relationship between Scotland and Bordeaux

The Politics of Wine in Britain: A New Cultural History by Charles Ludington
Palgrave Macmillan, 2013
A scholarly examination of how wine influenced British politics, culture and society over the centuries

A Yankee Jeffersonian: Selections from the Diary and Letters of William Lee of Massachusetts, Written from 1796 to 1840, ed Mary Lee Mann
Harvard University Press, 1958
Bordeaux and its wines through the eyes of an 18th-century American diplomat

Bordeaux Legends: The 1855 First Growth Wines of Haut-Brion, Lafite Rothschild, Latour, Margaux and Mouton Rothschild by Jane Anson
Editions de la Martinière, 2012
Anson was given unprecedented access to château archives for this seminal history

Château Chronicles

Château Lafite: The Almanac by Saskia de Rothschild
Flammarion, 2020
An engaging chronicle filled with personal stories, vintage notes and archival material by a scion of the dynasty, and head of Domaines Barons de Rothschild

Château de Fargues: The Incredible Ambition of the Lur Saluces Family in Sauternes by Hélène Farnault and François Poincet
Glenat, 2023
The often lurid story of the family which lost Château d'Yquem to LVMH in 2004, after 200 years in control of the great Sauternes estate

Château Clarke by Béatrice Brasseur and Georgie Hindle
Abrams, 2024
The Rothschild-owned property through the four seasons – Roots, Leaves, Flowers and Fruits – from past to future. Visually stunning

Politics, Economics and Scandal

Noble Rot: A Bordeaux Revolution by William Echikson
W W Norton & Co, 2006
The byzantine workings of the Bordeaux wine industry, focusing on the Lur Saluces family and Château d'Yquem

The Billionaire's Vinegar by Benjamin Wallace
Three Rivers Press, 2009
The convoluted story behind the multimillion dollar *cause célèbre* of the allegedly faked Jefferson bottles

Thirsty Dragon by Suzanne Mustacich
Henry Holt & Co, 2015
A detailed, insider's look at China's influence on Bordeaux's fine wine market. Essential reading

Reference

Inside Bordeaux by Jane Anson
Berry Bros & Rudd, 2020
Endowed with excellent maps, a look at
understanding Bordeaux through its
terroirs. *Inside Bordeaux* has quickly
become the authoritative book on
the region. A must for any serious
Bordeaux follower

*Bordeaux: The Wines, the Vineyards, the
Winemakers* by Oz Clarke
Pavilion, 2008
Exuberant, informative and entertaining
guide to the region, full of personal
anecdotes

*The Bordeaux Atlas and Encyclopaedia of
Châteaux* by Hubrecht Duijker and
Michael Broadbent
St Martin's Press, 1998
Weighty and authoritative, with pithy
description and clear maps by two
giants of wine; a favourite among
wine aficionados

The Complete Bordeaux Vintage Guide by
Neal Martin
Quadrille, 2023
150 years of Bordeaux vintages along with
cultural references – music, film and
other happenings – for each year

Biography, Anthology and Reflection

In the Vine Country by Edith Somerville and
Martin Ross
Académie du Vin Library, 2021
Two mischievously observant Anglo-Irish
ladies tour the Médoc in the 19th century.
A comic masterpiece

*Milady Vine: The autobiography of Baron
Philippe de Rothschild* written with Joan
Littlewood
Century Hutchinson, 1985
The late-in-life memoir of the racing driver,
poet, playwright, film producer
and Bordeaux grandee, who had a
tempestuous relationship with legendary
British theatre director Littlewood

From Bordeaux to the Stars by Jean-Michel
Cazes
Académie du Vin Library, 2023

Cazes' autobiography published shortly
before his death; pioneer of modern
Pauillac and one of Bordeaux's most-
loved figures

*The Secrets of My Life: Vintner, Prisoner,
Soldier, Spy* by Peter MF Sichel
Archway Publishing, 2016
Written at the age of 90, the memoir of
wine, espionage and adventure by a
legendary Bordeaux character

The Story of Wine: from Noah to Now by
Hugh Johnson
First published 1989, new ed Académie du
Vin Library, 2022
Bordeaux has more than 30 index entries
in Johnson's classic work. Chapters
cover the early châteaux, 'The age
of confidence', 'The golden age',
Napoleon, phylloxera and much more.
The perfect primer

On Bordeaux, ed Susan Keevil
Académie du Vin Library, 2021
A treasure-trove of essays and articles from
luminaries like Harry Waugh, Michael
Broadbent, Elie de Rothschild, Jean-
Michel Cazes and Steven Spurrier

A Village in the Vineyard by Thomas
Matthews and Sara Matthews
Farrar, Straus and Giroux, 1993
A charming and evocative account of
life in Entre-Deux-Mers by the former
Wine Spectator editor and his wife,
photographer Sara Matthews

Food and Wine

*The Wine & Food of Bordeaux and the South
West of France* by Ronan Sayburn
67 Pall Mall, 2022
A handsome volume on the wines of
Bordeaux with more than 50 recipes,
using local ingredients, to pair with them

*Lynch-Bages & Co: A family, a Wine & 52
Recipes* by Jean-Michel Cazes and
Jean-Luc Rocha
Glenat, 2013
The late Jean-Michel Cazes and Michelin-
starred chef Rocha draw on the history of
the family, the château and the region for
this blend of family memoir and gourmet
recipe book

Index

Acknowledgements

The publishers have made every effort to trace the copyright holders of the text and images reproduced in this book. If, however, you believe that any work has been incorrectly credited or used without permission, please contact us immediately and we will endeavour to rectify the situation.

Cover, 3 Shutterstock/Jilko, 1 Deepix.jpg, 4bl, 28 Cephas, 4br, 45 Philippe Roy, 6-7 Philippe Roy/CIVB, 8 Brice Braastad, 14 CIVB, 22 Edwin Remsberg/Alamy Stock Photo, 25 C. Y. Yu/South China Morning Post via Getty Images, 26 ANAKA, 34-35 Shutterstock/Sergii Figurnyi, 36 Pierre Plan-chenault, 40 CIVB, 42 Shutterstock/FreeProd33, 43 Shutterstock/barmalini, 44 robertharding/Alamy Stock Photo, 48 Shutterstock/sylv1rob1, 52 Shutterstock/Arnieby, 66-67 Jean-Pierre Lamarque, 68 Anne-Emmanuelle Thion, 70 CIVB, 76 CIVB, 80 Château Mouton-Rothschild, 81 Dme de Chevalier, 82 Hemis/Alamy Stock Photo, 88-89 UGCB, 90 Shutterstock/Sergey Kelin, 92 Shutterstock/Richard Semik, 94 Shutterstock/That French Bloke, 97 Creative Commons, 98 Shutterstock/FreeProd33, 101 Shutterstock/ SpiritProd33, 102 CIVB, 110 Shutterstock/sylv1rob1, 116-117 CIVB, 118 Daniel Cathiard, 121b Shutterstock/ Peter Titmuss, 123t Shutterstock/ Oliverouge 3, 123b Shutterstock/E. Cowez, 125 Anne Lanta, 134 Celestin Coutaud, 140t L'atelier de style, 148 Raphael Zimmermann Oryx Photo, 151 Maison Nouvelle, 153 G Bonnaud, 155bl Soif Bordeaux, 156 Buvette Bordeaux, 157t G Bonnaud, 158 Cave de la Gironde Bordeaux, 163b Celestin Coutaud, 166 Anne-Emmanuelle Thion, 167 Nicolas Bouriette, 171 Sous la Robe, 173 Au Bon Jaja, 180 Shutterstock/riekephotos
Images of businesses are copyright of those businesses.

Also available in
The Smart Traveller's Wine Guide series

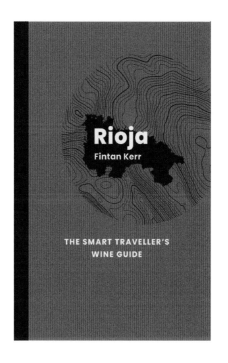

and coming soon...
Napa | Tuscany | Rhône | Switzerland

Other books from Académie du Vin
Library we think you'll enjoy

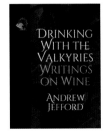

www.academieduvinlibrary.com